A
FOUNDATION
for Life

—A GRANDFATHER'S WISDOM

A FOUNDATION *for Life*

—A GRANDFATHER'S WISDOM

Dear Richard,

*May you add
these words to
your own wisdom.*

Worth M. Helms

Worth M. Helms

Interior Layout and Design by
Julie Csizmadia (julicsiz@hotmail.com)

*Dedicated to my grandchildren Worth IV and Lily
and any future additions.*

ACKNOWLEDGMENTS

. . . .

A significant part of this book is attributable to lessons learned from a number of people in my life. My father, Worth M. Helms Sr., and mother, Nancy K. Helms, were very good teachers and role models in terms of hard work, values, and self-discipline. They taught as much by example as they did verbally. My wife Janet continues to teach me every day what it means to have faith, patience, and constant relationship. Our son, Trey Helms, and my sister, Carolyn Wyland, are sources of experiences from which I learn and teach. Special thanks to our daughter-in-law Cameron for entering Trey's life and delivering our beautiful grandchild! And Olivia, our spiritual daughter in Uganda, has added unexpected depth to our lives.

Others have made observations or introduced me to or guided me through circumstances that have dramatically altered my perspective on how to handle life's issues. Lt. Col. Cesar, General Billy Thomas, and MSgt Charles Claussen in the US Army in the 1960's were instrumental in leading me in my military experience. Dr. Richard Levin at UNC-CH saw something in me and hired me to subcontract some consulting work in the late 60's. Jack Conroy and V.A. Ballard were my first bosses at Springs Mills and reoriented me to the business world and civilian life. Franklin W. Bowen was my senior business partner for 17 years and totally rerouted my career path and financial future. Dr. Nicholas Hanna was an advisor and mentor as I pursued education in the counseling field in the 90's. The Stuart Coffee Club in Stuart Florida receives credit for the germ of the idea behind this book.

My gratitude to each and every one of you and many others who have passed through my life and from whom I have learned many of the lessons contained herein. I stand today on your shoulders. Thank you.

TABLE OF CONTENTS

. . . .

INTRODUCTION

. . . .

"I'm going to be your Grandpa, I have this biggest smile
I've been waiting to meet you, for such a long, long while."

These words from Billy Crystal say exactly what I felt as our family eagerly awaited the birth of our first grandchild in 2011. I did not expect to feel so joyful and elated at the birth of a new life and generation, but it completed my circle of life. Eighteen months later our second grandchild was born.

This book began in February of 2010 when a friend in a discussion group asked me what three things I would like to teach my grandchildren. Although at age 67 I had no grandchildren, and my son, Trey, was 34 and well on his own, the question intrigued me since I hoped to have grandkids some day. I began collecting ideas and principles from my memory of things that I have been taught or learned through experience and tried to practice during my lifetime that might be valuable to our next generation. In June of 2010 I realized Trey, even though he was 34, still had lots of stages of life to experience that I had already been through, and if I wrote these observations for him, he might find them helpful. I became a little more serious about the project. Then in March of 2011 he and his wife Cameron announced they were expecting, and this cast a whole new light on the issue. I began to get really serious about it, because now there was another generation who might benefit from my sometimes hard-earned lessons.

I then began to cast my net a little farther because it occurred to me that some of the lessons I've learned might be useful to others. For example, I mentor a couple of people and have a wide array of relationships who might benefit from the concepts included herein. You probably have the same situation, so the book is for everyone, not just grandparents.

Many people probably know a lot of what is presented here but have never articulated these "Blocks" to themselves. Reading these wisdom points may help crystallize them further and give them more "stickiness". It is my hope you find this helpful personally and in teaching others.

What you hold in your hands is a capsule of 69 years of living, learning, mistakes, successes, joy, sadness, and a host of other words that describe our human experience. When I was in Officer Candidate School in 1967, a friend and I had a great debate. He argued that it would be wonderful if people could learn instantly life's lessons from others through telepathy or some sort of mind-meld process. I held that it was better for people to learn through their own experiences. Well, Dave Klousie, it is 44 years later and after that long road, I've come around to your viewpoint. A lot of pain and anguish would be avoided if we could learn intuitively from the experiences of others. But since most of us haven't reached the telepathy stage of communication, we'll have to settle for the written word to benefit from their experience and wisdom. This is my written word to those willing to take the time to read it. I stand on the shoulders of those who have come before me, and I hope to help you to help others stand on your shoulders.

I've been a student, an Army officer, a business owner, a parent, a husband, a board member in a number of non-profit organizations, travelled world wide, experienced 8 mission trips to Africa, made money, lost money, made great decisions, and made lousy decisions. I've had lots of opportunities to learn lessons, and have had to take remedial courses in some of those life lessons several

INTRODUCTION

times. I've just become a mentor for a jail inmate, and I think I'll learn as much as he will. Learning never stops.

Where did the title originate? During the writing of this book, someone asked what part of a house I would want to be. I briefly sifted through all the parts --door, window, floor, basement, roof, attic, etc-- and then it hit me that the question was related to the development of this book. It's about building a *foundation* for living and accomplishing fulfillment, joy, success, and all the other things most of us desire to have a life well-lived during our time on earth. It's also about making wise decisions and avoiding pain, so that's why I call the book "A Foundation for Life".

A home's foundation often consists of cement blocks which support the home, so each of the concepts herein is called a "Block". Cemented together and integrated with each other, these blocks create a foundation for living and guidelines that support your life. I have not gone into exhaustive detail about each of these to justify them, although many pages could be written about most of them. I was concerned that prattling on would become too preachy. Many of the "Blocks" have corollaries to emphasize them and to help you remember them.

My lessons aren't over yet and I don't have anything close to the wisdom available to me, but many of the "Blocks" are things I have gleaned through experience to date, conversations with other experienced people, or mentors of my own. If I had practiced all of them all the time, I could have avoided a lot of anguish, loss, retrenchment, and some difficult situations in which I put myself. As a loving grandparent, parent or friend, you would probably like to help those in your circle avoid these same difficulties. Some of these are things you can still mention to your kids, even if they are parents. My sincerest wish is that you can take enough of these to heart to help those you mentor to avoid some of the errors many of us make.

13

A FOUNDATION FOR LIFE

I have several suggestions for your use of these observations:

1. Don't read them all at once. Read them slowly, ponder them and consider whether you think they are valid. You'll have to chew on some of them to determine if they fit within your belief and value system. Some will probably challenge you, but consider them even-handedly.

2. If, after due deliberation, you feel a "Block" is something you can honor as a truth you would like to teach, write how you feel about it and how you would like to help your offspring or others put it into practice.

3. Try to weave the "block" into your behavior, too. It will only have validity for those you are trying to teach if you practice it yourself. After all, you can't teach others something you don't model for them. Children (and friends) aren't just watching you, they are *absorbing* you. Our primary responsibility as grandparents/parents/mentors is to be what we hope our grandchildren/children/mentees will become. Remember, as much is caught as is taught, and that begs the question, what are you throwing? These "Blocks" will operate as does your autonomic nervous system which enables functions of the body to continue without conscious thought (heartbeat, breathing, etc.) If you think about them, and consciously remind yourself of them, they will become automatic.

4. Decide how, when, and to whom you would like to talk about these concepts. There are some examples in the Appendix of language to use to teach younger children.

5. Take your time with this, but don't delay it. Occasionally review the "Blocks" to reinforce their validity. Reiterate these lessons with your progeny periodically. Some of these

have "stickiness", enabling them to stick quickly. Others will take more time and practice. Life is a marathon, not a sprint. Keep at it.

6. Use this as a workbook. Write in the margin who you would like to teach it to and when you plan to teach it.

Just because I am becoming a grandfather and hope to teach these "Blocks" to my grandchild doesn't mean they are exclusive to grandfathers. They apply to grandmothers as well, and to granddaughters as well as grandsons. They apply to young parents as well as to older grandparents. Erik Erikson was a psychologist who proposed that there are eight seasons during your life. The last season he defines as "Generativity" or the time when you pass on to others the wisdom you have. This book is intended to help you do that, and, irrespective of your age, I believe that contained herein are timeless truths that apply to everyone.

Many of these observations are not very easy to practice, and sometimes human nature will intrude and cause us to violate them. Some of these you will already practice. Some you will unconsciously know but never will have verbalized to yourself. But I believe they can be valuable to you as you try to grow and teach others to be better kids, better spouses, better bosses, better co-workers, better parents, better citizens. We need good citizens to keep our country great.

My original challenge was to determine what I would want to teach my son and my grandchildren. Whichever of these lessons or behaviors you decide to adopt into your own code, those are the ones you will be modeling for those around you, whether family or not. They may even be helpful to you yourself. We teach what we are.

What's the difference between knowledge and wisdom? Knowledge is information, facts, data, statistics, etc. Wisdom is the ability to astutely, perceptively, and with good judgment apply that knowledge. My favorite metaphor of this is "Knowledge is being aware that a tomato is a fruit. Wisdom is knowing you don't put tomatoes in fruit salad".

I hope you've read this far because my last point is really important, maybe the most important one in the book. There are many attributes and behaviors that enable people to lead enriched, fulfilled, and secure lives. At the forefront of the ability to accomplish these are self-awareness and consciousness.

I define self-awareness as your ability to honestly evaluate yourself and your behavior, actions, and impact on your surroundings. It involves introspection and candid self-evaluation about how you think, talk, and behave. Self-awareness is inner-directed.

I define consciousness as your ability to observe the impact you are having on the world around you and adjusting your behavior, words, and actions to have a thoughtful influence. Consciousness is outer-directed.

If you purposefully practice these two skills, and combine them with some of the nuggets you will find herein, I believe you will position those you love and care about to more capably deal with life and its challenges.

Good luck and God Speed on the journey!

ONE

Communications

....

"Take advantage of every opportunity to practice your communication skills so that when important occasions arise, you will have the gift, the style, the sharpness, the clarity and the emotions to affect other people."
— JIM ROHN

BLOCK 1. The words you choose to deliver your message are as important as the tone of voice with which they are delivered, and the connotation of words is as important as the denotation. The message you deliver will be soft or harsh depending upon the words you select to deliver it.

For example, rather than saying, "Stop talking so loudly!", you could say, "Would you mind speaking a little more softly?". The message is the same but the tone is much softer, and it's less likely to create an adversarial reaction. Words can isolate and anger the receiver or convince him/her to be on your side.

Once I was entering a jail to visit someone and had left a form at home that was required to enter the jail for security purposes. I could have said, "I've traveled all the way here. I've visited before. You just have to let me in so I don't waste a trip." But instead I said, "Officer Jones (people love to hear their name and title acknowledged), I just totally forgot the form at home. It's my responsibility for doing that, and if you are unable to let me pass, I will understand and accept your decision and will come the next time with the correct paperwork. If there's anything you can do to help me, though, I will deeply appreciate it and will promise to not make a habit of this."

I acknowledged his power and control (which was the reality) and asked for help. Asking for help is a very powerful request that is difficult to refuse. I gave up nothing, except a little ego, and I have a good enough sense of self and confidence so that that part of me will grow back! He extended himself by making a call and letting me enter. Soft words work. Remember to use them.

Corollary: *Practice keeping your words soft and sweet just in case you have to eat them.*

Corollary: *You can always step up the harshness of your message, but start out soft since harsh is difficult to retract and stings and attacks the recipient. If you begin harshly, you can't retract it and it's harder to negotiate.*

Corollary: *Control your tongue and you control your circumstances.*

Corollary: *It only takes a few seconds to open profound wounds in others and sometimes a lifetime to heal them.*

BLOCK 2. You have two ears and one mouth. Use them in that ratio and people will develop confidence in you and trust you. Listeners are highly valued in business and personal relationships.

The best salesman I ever met asked me lots of questions, quietly listened, and made good eye contact as I responded. Many of my responses prompted more questions. At the end of an hour he had turned himself into a trusted confidant and knew everything he needed to know to tell me how his product addressed the issues I had revealed in response to his questions. It wasn't manipulative. He was genuinely interested in what I had to say.

This is valuable in every communication, including personal situations. I began doing a lot more listening and asking questions in both my personal and business relationships and the results were tangible. The best way I know to actively listen is to ask yourself occasional questions in the middle of a conversation. "How much am I listening to this person? What question can I ask to glean more information about this topic? How engaged is this person in the conversation? How can I make this conversation more about the other person?" By asking yourself questions about your listening skills, you become more conscious of them and this sharpens those skills.

Another positive aspect of listening is once the other person has been allowed to talk out his/her information and feelings, they are much more willing to listen to and hear your input. I began getting feedback like "I feel comfortable talking to you", or "I feel I can trust you", or "I don't know why I'm talking so much".

Of course, for you to be listening, the other person must be talking, and the very best way to accomplish this is to ask questions. Each answer someone gives to a question almost invariably leads to another question you can ask to enable you to continue the listening process. You can also encourage the person to continue talking by nodding your head, or saying "Yes", or "Really?", or "Interesting", or "Could you tell me a little more about that?".

Caveat: *Be sure you honor the trust they have placed in you by maintaining their confidences, and treating the relationship with integrity. Listen twice as much as you speak and you will become a trusted counselor, a more highly valued friend, and a more informed and wiser person.*

Corollary: *When in doubt, ask a question.*

Corollary: *Use open-ended questions (not closed-ended ones that can be answered with "Yes" or "No"). Open-ended questions must be answered with explanations, and are conversation creators that lead to other questions. Closed-ended questions are conversation killers. Open ended questions often begin with the words Who, What, When, Why, or How.*

Corollary: *If you are talking, you are not learning.*

BLOCK 3. Look closely at people's behavior to confirm the truth of their words.

When people's words are not consistent with their actions, behavior, or decisions, an alarm bell should ring in your head. Congruence between the two is critical for integrity to exist in that person and for trust to be deserved. Look to behavior as the bell weather of how deep you want your relationship to go with people and how safe you feel trusting them.

For example, if someone tells you they are your friend and want to help you, and then they ridicule you or tease you mercilessly in front of others, you might question the truth of their words. The most egregious example of this is when someone says they love you and then verbally or physically abuses you. Whole books are written about this particular behavior. Sometimes someone will be passive-aggressive and resist you by secretly undermining the relationship with actions and then trying to smooth it over with words. If you find yourself experiencing any of these relationships, evaluate how beneficial the relationship is to you and whether you want to continue it on that basis, or confront the behavior to try to change the dynamic. If confronting the behavior doesn't change the dynamic, strongly consider terminating the relationship since it may not be headed in a healthy direction.

Corollary: *Liars figure and figures lie.*

Corollary: *Actions speak louder than words*

BLOCK 4. Don't judge the opinions or input of others too quickly. Avoid the maxim "Often in Error, Never in Doubt". Remember—sometimes you're wrong or only half right.

Take time to hear the other person's viewpoint. There may be a middle ground between your two views that is more effective. Perhaps there is merit in each position and a merger of the two will create a stronger position or answer. Don't be so wedded to an idea just because it is your idea that you are rigid in your defense of it. This is a great place to use that listening skill you developed.

> **Corollary:** *You can accomplish a lot more and have less conflict when nobody cares who gets the credit.*

> **Corollary:** *The whole can be greater than the sum of the parts.*

BLOCK 5. Don't try to be the first to respond to a question just to make an impression. Better to deliberate a little with yourself, then respond.

A friend of mine went to Japan to teach. It was uncomfortable for him at first because when he asked a question of the class, it took 30 or so seconds for someone to raise a hand. He was accustomed to people immediately answering to show how sharp and quick they were. He was told that in Japan students consider what they are going to say before they respond in order to challenge themselves. We have a tendency in America to say the first thing that pops into our minds rather than deliberating with ourselves first. When you say the first thing you think of, you may be painting yourself into a corner that you have to defend that is not so defensible. Think before you speak.

I actually experienced this once in a class. A professor asked a question and several hands shot up. He called on three or four other people while I sat and thought. I finally raised my hand and gave the answer I had developed and he nodded as I responded. He later hired me for a summer internship because I thought before I spoke and yet had had the courage to give an answer that disagreed with everyone else.

Corollary: *Never put both feet in your mouth at the same time, because then you won't have a leg to stand on.*

TWO

Conducting Yourself

....

*"By constant self discipline and self control you can
develop greatness of character."*
—GRENVILLE KLEISER

BLOCK 1. Mistakes in our lives are often the result of errors in judgment or bad decisions. Deliberate and pray long and hard about significant decisions, and give extra weight to your gut feel about a decision. Your instincts often may be more accurate than your analytical skills. MOST IMPORTANTLY, if you are not AT PEACE with a decision, if there are still significant pangs of doubt, take more time until you come to peace.

Someone once told me, "Emotion is the master, logic is the slave", meaning that emotion often drives our decisions and then we use our logic to justify them. If you sense that a decision you are making is not right, but you tell yourself "Here is the rationale that justifies the decision", you may be letting this mistake prevail. I have made decisions from emotional motivations that I subconsciously knew were wrong, but my logic justified them. I didn't listen to my gut, and I failed to do what I call "asserting myself with myself". Don't fall into this trap. Quietly praying (or meditating if you don't want to use the word praying) will help you get to your gut feeling more than any amount of thought. Note: Emotional motivations are sneaky. You may think you are making a rational decision but you need to look very hard to determine what is really driving the decision.

I once decided to invest a significant amount of money with a manager. I did a lot of research that made everything look okay, and, although I never felt comfortable (at peace) with the decision, I invested anyway. Ultimately I lost all the money. Had I deliberated longer until I was at peace, I may well have been better off.

Second, make <u>sure</u> you have all the facts and information before you begin evaluating your decision. I know people who react powerfully and emotionally to every circumstance they encounter and they never take the time to gather the facts before making a decision. They rarely make good decisions and often have to reverse course or live with difficult outcomes. Be sure you drill deep when collecting your facts. Double check your sources of answers. I've been in situations where people have told me what they thought I wanted to hear, or what they wanted me to hear, or what they thought were the facts but were wrong. Always corroborate your answer to reconcile the info you obtain.

Third, I have failed way too often to bring a trusted person into my thinking and evaluation process when I was considering a decision. When you talk about an issue out loud with someone else, it brings a different characterization and clarity to the issue than when you ruminate about it in your own mind. It is rare when you can think about all the implications and angles by yourself. Having a trusted person ask you questions, explore possibilities, and evaluate your feelings about an issue will add an invaluable resource to your self-deliberations.

When you ask this person to help you think through an issue, ask them to do the following:

1. Don't begin by giving me advice about the issue.

2. Instead, ask me questions to help me think of things I haven't considered.

3. Help me think of additional options that I might explore.

4. Ask me questions that help me get to the feelings I have about the issue, and help me identify any alarm bells I hear faintly or loudly ringing.

5. I came to you because I trust you and I'm making myself vulnerable by confiding in you. Please honor that trust by keeping our conversation confidential.

My dad died at my age 26. I wish he had been around for me to bounce things off of. I'm honored that our son calls me regularly to help him evaluate decisions, and I try to do it in the way I have outlined above.

Fourth, a technique my sister reminded me of is the old T-square method. Draw a line down the center of a sheet of paper. On the left write the positive (rewards) reasons for taking the action, and on the right note the negative (risks). Take several days to do this so the various implications have time to percolate to the surface in your brain. At the end of that time you will probably have most of the pros and cons down and the decision will be fairly obvious.

Now reverse your role and assume you are the person who has been asked for advice. Advise in a manner that does not fix responsibility for the advice on you. If you tell them what to do and the outcome is negative, you are at least secondarily and maybe primarily responsible for the outcome. Whether you are primarily or secondarily responsible depends on the conviction with which you advise the advice seeker. There could even be legal consequences to giving your advice.

How do you avoid putting yourself in this situation? Simply apply the above rules to yourself and communicate this to the advice seeker. Tell him/her the guidelines under which you agree to help them develop a response to the situation for which they are seeking advice:

1. I won't tell you what to do;

2. I'll ask questions to help you think of all the considerations you need to evaluate;

3. I'll help you think of all your options;

4. I'll try to help you identify the feelings you have about the issue and what your concerns are; and

5. I will keep our discussion confidential.

If the person insists and says, "I really want to know what you think I should do", the appropriate thing to say is "Let's stick to the process, and I think the answer will reveal itself to you, and won't place too much emphasis on my opinion." This also teaches them a healthy process to use in the future about decisions.

Of course, all the above must be leavened with consideration of the advisee's age. The younger they are, the more guidance and direction you will give them in terms of advice. You can use the process for a six year old to teach decision making skills, but the final say is yours.

Corollary: *Listen to your gut, trust your instincts.*

Corollary: *Your biggest enemy in making decisions will be impatience. Take your time. The helter-skelter world will try to rush you to a decision. Don't. Years of planning and thinking happened before the first stone was laid for the pyramids.*

Corollary: *Two heads are better than one.*

Corollary: *Don't believe everything you hear.*

Corollary: *Wisdom chooses to do now what it knows will satisfy it later (Joyce Myers)*

Corollary: *Freedom to make decisions is always accompanied by responsibility for the outcome of those decisions.*

Corollary: *Trust but verify.*

BLOCK 2. Here is how the meaning and value of your life will unfold:

Your thoughts will determine your words.

Your words will determine your actions.

Your actions will determine your habits.

Your habits will determine your character.

Your character will determine your destiny.

Notice what lies at the root of this sequence: thought. The one thing that has enabled mankind to carve a different presence on Earth than that of animals is thought. Everything we have, our possessions, our games, our entertainment, our institutions, our jobs, how we relate to others, etc, is based on our ability to think and ideate.

You can extend this not only to our technological, scientific, and material accomplishments but also to our personal behavior. In psychology a concept was evolved years ago by Aaron T. Beck called cognitive behavioral theory. He believed that your thoughts and beliefs determine your behavior and your responses. Your thoughts and beliefs are programmed into you by the experiences you have had throughout your life. If your behavior is undesirable or unhealthy, you can change it by changing your beliefs and thoughts. The problem with this is that most of us are pretty comfortable where we are, even if it is unhealthy, and don't want to change or don't even know we need to change.

If you want to change anything in your circumstances (how you relate to others, your habits, your financial well-being and so forth), you must have the courage to examine your belief system and the effect it is having on you. For example, if you were "taught" that education is not a worthwhile pursuit, and you don't even receive a high school diploma, the likelihood of a solid financial future is dim. You have to change that belief system. If you are taught through your relationship with your father that males are not to be trusted, you will have a difficult time having a healthy relationship with a spouse. Examining your belief system will help you determine how you can re-program your thoughts to change your perspective and your outcomes.

If you want to change your circumstances, if you want to change how you respond to situations, if you want to change how you behave, examine how you think and what you believe. You will create a different sequence as outlined above and that will change the outcome and that will change your destiny.

Corollary: *One of the biggest determinants of what you think is what you read. Choose carefully.*

BLOCK 3. The events of your life may be there because you have drawn them to you by your actions or your words, or they just happened. Often you have no control over those events. What you can control is your response to those events. What happens to you may be painful or rewarding, but the most important thing is how you respond to it.

In 2005 an oncologist cheerfully announced to me that I had a 3" pharangeal tumor in my throat. She wasn't being irrational with the way she delivered the news, she was just being upbeat. I give you my word that within about 15 seconds, the thought crossed my mind that I was in a win-win situation. I was either going to die and return home, or I was going to live and have more time with my loved ones. I spent a lot of time in physical misery the next five months with chemo, radiation, double pneumonia, and pleurisy, but I spent only about 5 hours one day being depressed about my circumstances. As someone said to me later, I seemed to float above it.

Conversely, in 1990 my partners and I had a huge business success. It was one of the largest insurance cases written that year for a corporation. We felt great about it, and celebrated a little bit, but the next day I was back in the office making phone calls to new prospects. I knew unless I kept working on filling the pipeline, the next success would be a long time coming.

It's not what happens to you that is most important. It's how you respond that makes the biggest difference.

Corollary: *Attitude is the most important determinant of how you respond to the challenges and successes life presents to you.*

Corollary: *Live in vision, not in circumstance.*

Musing: *I know God doesn't give me anything I can't handle. Sometimes, though, I wish he just didn't trust me so much.*

BLOCK 4. Always stand for what is right. Don't follow the crowd if you disagree with the values that stand behind their words and actions. The herd mentality is often wrong, and you may be the cowboy or cowgirl who can change the direction of the herd.

I was once a member of Rotary International, a marvelous service organization. Rotary has as its mantra what they call a four way test to apply to anything you think, say, or do: "Is it the truth?" "Is it fair to all concerned?" "Will it build goodwill and better friendships?" and "Will it be beneficial to all concerned?" We would all do well to follow this practice.

This one, of course, raises the question of what is right. What's right is determined by the standards of your value system and by the impact your actions have on others, positive or negative. Another answer to what is right is, would you do it if your mother was watching?

When I was about 9, I returned home one afternoon from playing in a neighbor's yard. My mother noticed a toy that she had not purchased and asked where I obtained it. I said "I saw it in Peter's yard and picked it up and brought it home. I "borrowed" it." "Did you ask permission", she asked. "Well, no" I replied. She walked to the phone, called Peter's mother, and asked her to watch for me because I would be coming over to return a toy I had misappropriated from her yard. That little dose of healthy shame gave me an everlasting respect for other people's property.

I had to re-learn this lesson at age 17 when Mom required me to return a bath towel and an ash tray I had taken from a hotel on a high school band trip to the Gator Bowl, even though all the other band members did the same thing. It just wasn't right for me to take things that were not mine, no matter how incon-sequential. And by the way, if the test of knowing something is wrong by whether you would want your mother to know about it isn't powerful enough for you, try the test of whether you would want God to know about it.

Corollary: *Don't do anything just to be part of the crowd, even if you have to leave the crowd behind.*

Corollary: *Whenever you are doing something you are not proud of or would not want your mother to know about, stop it.*

Corollary: *Without courage, all other attributes are meaningless. (Winston Churchill)*

BLOCK 5. Use healthfully applied ambition to better the lot of yourself and those around you.

Ambition is a good thing as long as it is leavened with consideration for the feelings and well-being of others. My favorite example of bad ambition is the recordings of the energy traders at Enron making jokes about how they were gouging the public with their manipulation of energy prices in California. They were making money hand over fist all the while knowing they were abusing people in the process. That's unhealthy ambition personified. Don't do it. If you use your ambition to better the lot of others or of organizations, you will be rewarded.

BLOCK 6. Persistence is the most important quality to practice when you are in the midst of difficult times or difficult projects.

Life is often brutal. Sometimes it's hard to remember that the battle you are fighting and the effort you are making will have a result and an end point. Remember to look up at the horizon occasionally to re-kindle your courage and hope and to redouble your effort to accomplish your goal or to fight your way out of a mess.

Although persistence is extremely important it should be constantly leavened with reason. Is there a better way to reach the goal? What forces can I bring to bear that I haven't considered? Persistence is one of my three most important behaviors to practice. I'll tell you my others as we go.

Corollary: *Keep hope alive.*

Corollary: *This too shall pass.*

Corollary: *Keep your eye on the horizon while fighting the alligators at your feet.*

Corollary: *Never, never, never give up. (Winston Churchill)*

Corollary: *Success comes not only from being dealt a good hand, but also from playing a poor hand well.*

Corollary: *Remember the lessons you learned from the past but process the pain until you can put it behind you. Face the present with your new found knowledge.*

Corollary: *Focus on your hopes and dreams of the future and strain forward to what lies ahead.*

BLOCK 7. Do everything you can to practice compassion, love, and consideration for others. Always consider the work-a-day person: the secretary, the janitor, the doorman, etc. If you give them recognition and are cheerful with them, they'll stand for you when you need it, and they'll feel better about themselves. This is the second of my three most important characteristics.

Everyone has a place in this world, and if you acknowledge that person and his/her existence, it will brighten their day. You'll feel good about yourself for having done it, too. And if you ever need help, they will be the first to cheerfully assist you.

Corollary: *Leaven your decisions and actions with compassion, and you will never have to say I'm sorry.*

Corollary: *Do the same for street people. There but for the Grace of God go you.*

Corollary: *You may be only one person in the world, but you may also be the world to one person.*

Corollary: *Life is like an echo. You will get back what you put in. (This was told to me by the inmate I am mentoring. I told you I would learn from him.)*

Corollary: *The measure of a man is what he does for people who can do nothing for him.*

BLOCK 8. Treat life with a sense of humor. Laughter has healing power and makes life so much more fun and zestful. It also helps you not take yourself or your circumstances quite so seriously.

Endorphins are released every time you laugh, and endorphins heal you physically and emotionally. Generate them by laughing and heal yourself. Life is a lot more fun if you approach it looking for the cheer rather than the dour side. It will lend a quality of lightness to your life that will make the tough times easier to negotiate.

Corollary: *Laughter is the best medicine.*

BLOCK 9. Always be on time. It shows respect for other people's time and effort and tells them you have good self-discipline.

This is as much about courtesy and consideration for others as it is about good time management and efficiency. Others have schedules, too, and have made time in theirs for me, so the least I can do in return is to be prompt. I take it to the extreme of believing if I am on time, I'm late. I'd rather wait for the other person than have them wait for me.

Corollary: *You will manage your time as well as you respect the time of others.*

BLOCK 10. Drive carefully. It's not only cars that can be recalled by their maker.

In an instant, your pleasurable driving of that vehicle you so enjoy and are proud of can transform traumatically into assault with a deadly weapon. Tailgating, DUI, driving carelessly, speeding, phoning, texting, etc. can all turn you and your victims into tragic figures for a lifetime. Focus on your driving when you are in your car, and don't let distractions cause you or others a lifetime of agony or even death.

BLOCK 11. Leave behind you what I call an audit trail of integrity. Say what you will do and do what you say with good will toward men. Tell the truth, even when you are wrong, or it embarrasses you, or it causes you to have to correct an error you have made. You'll never have to worry about looking in the mirror. This is third of the three most important characteristics.

This cannot be overemphasized. Integrity is the most important element of how you conduct yourself. It determines whether you are trusted or not. It determines how you feel about yourself and whether your self-image is healthy. Without integrity people will always be suspicious of your motives. Your reputation depends upon your integrity. Let your name stand for honor and truth. You will always be able to look yourself in the eye and say, "I did what was right."

Not lying is where integrity starts. A synonym for integrity is honesty, so integrity continues with objective evaluation and telling people disadvantages as well as advantages of things you propose. Giving people bad information unintentionally is not lying, but you need to correct it as soon as possible. Calling someone and saying "I was wrong" gives you credibility and is the right thing to do.

Corollary: *If you don't lie, you don't have to remember what you said.*

BLOCK 12. The second mouse gets the cheese. Be cautiously aggressive.

If you are too aggressive you may overreach and, if you aren't aggressive enough, you may not achieve your dreams. It's difficult to determine the correct amount of aggression. But if you always try to give 110% of your effort, it will probably be about right. On the other hand, some of my most important life lessons have come from being too aggressive and failing. Evaluate the risks and if the commensurate rewards are worth it, go for it. Don't allow fear of failure to rule your aggression.

There are several types of risks in life to evaluate as you are determining how aggressive you want to be. The areas that I can think of in which I need to assess the risk in order to determine how aggressive I want to be are physical risks, financial risks, health risks, relationship risks, emotional risks, and spiritual risks. When you are contemplating decisions in any of these areas, you are doing so in a way that tries to define the worst things that can happen (downside risk) and the upside potential (rewards or gains).

Here's an example. I once decided I wanted to have the experience of jumping from an airplane (with a parachute, of course!). In coming to that decision, I evaluated the downside (I could be injured a little or a lot or I could even die). I also evaluated how I could offset that risk with the training I would receive, the support from the instructors, and the communications from the ground to me while I was in the air (instructions via one-way radio). I also thought about why I wanted to do this: to prove to myself I had the physical and mental courage to do something that few people dare to attempt. My emotional need to prove something to myself outweighed the dangers and I trained for about seven hours and jumped. I actually was injured and had to do some therapy, but to this day I am glad I made the decision. My emotional need was so strong that, even in light of the risks, I made a decision that in the cold hard light of day was not really rational.

Had I not had such a strong need to prove something to myself, I would not have done it. My emotional drivers overrode my rationality. That's okay, as long as you can define and know the reason you know you are making a decision. My payback in this case was enhanced confidence and courage to tackle other things in my life.

The same is true of decisions we make in the other defined areas above. We make decisions every day that involve finances, health, relationships, emotions, and our spiritual selves. The point here is to be intentional about assessing the risks and knowing the reason you are making decisions.

> **BLOCK 13.** Nobody cares if you can't dance well. They're worried enough about how they look, so just get up and dance.

Ever see someone who you thought wasn't dancing very smoothly but looked like he/she was having a really good time? I don't think I'm a very good dancer, although my wife, Janet, insists I am to encourage me to get her on the dance floor. I've always admired those people for having the pluck to get out there and just have fun. Let go and enjoy yourself. That's why the band is playing. And, of course, you could always take some dance lessons. And if you are married to or dating a person who loves to dance, take the initiative to ask them out on the dance floor. They will deeply appreciate it and love you more for it.

BLOCK 14. Don't try or not try—do or don't do.

How often have you heard someone say "I'll try to do so and so"? It's a nice thing to say, but it doesn't go far enough. It is not nearly as much of a commitment as it is to say "I **will** do so and so". To say "I will" rather than "I'll try" is a much more positive statement of commitment to a goal. As a famous advertisement says, "Just do it".

Corollary: *Never, never, never give up. You've heard this before.*

BLOCK 15. If something has gone wrong, first look in the mirror to see if the cause lies there.

This will come as a shock to you, but neither you nor I is perfect! I can be wrong, and you can too, and it's important to recognize that. When you are in the midst of conflict, look in the mirror to evaluate what your role is and whether you might be the cause. Don't be so thin-skinned and egocentric to refuse to admit to yourself and others that you are wrong. Conscious and intentional introspection is an invaluable tool to measure your impact on others, to evaluate the validity of your decisions, and to initiate course corrections that are necessary to keep you headed in the right direction.

Introspection creates a continuous feedback loop for you to evaluate yourself in all the circumstances and roles you play. It is absolutely essential if you are going to grow as a person and to be effective in whatever you are doing. Without it, you are on autopilot and are just reacting to what is happening in your environment. Autopilot doesn't allow you to decide whether to change course or not. Speakers continuously observe their audiences to monitor how they are responding so they can adjust to their audience's reactions. You can do the same thing to judge the impact of your words, your decisions, and your interactions with others.

In 1992 my second wife and I agreed we did not have the energy to continue to try to make our relationship work. Shortly thereafter I was thinking about the fact that I now had two failed attempts at marriage and I was the common thread between them. It was time for me to look at the role I played in the marriages and to determine what I needed to do to recast the framework with which I approached marriage. I did not do this by going to a counselor but by enrolling in a Masters degree in counseling. Over the next two years I did a great deal of introspection as a part of obtaining the degree and discovered some things about myself that I needed to reframe. Significant changes came about and I changed direction.

Accountability is one of the most difficult things for our egos to deal with, but unless we "hold our feet to the fire" we'll never get better at what we are doing. There are times I don't like doing this because it wounds my ego. But every time I do it the result is positive.

Corollary: *The truth will set you free, but first it will make you miserable.*

Corollary: *Would you rather fight to be right when you are wrong, or be happy?*

Corollary: *Freedom is commensurate with self-responsibility.*

Corollary: *If you lie to yourself, you are more likely to lie to others.*

Corollary: *People get in the most trouble when they are not honest with themselves.*

> **BLOCK 16.** The truth you speak has no past and no future. It is and that's all it needs to be.

Truth might be defined simply as recognition of reality. Truth is timeless. Principles are timeless. But we humans seem to be unable to learn lessons from our predecessors. We can view their mistakes through history, but then we repeat the same mistakes. We think we can do anything we want regardless of the ethics or morality involved and there will be no consequences. We believe we can remove faith from our lives and there will be no consequences. But no nation in the history of Earth has remained strong and righteous when it lost sight of basic principles and ethics as a societal norm. Truth is timeless.

Corollary: *Economic and political freedom rely upon the composite self-discipline of a nation.*

BLOCK 17. Live your life with as much intentionality as you can muster.

Intentionality is, in my opinion, one of the most important habits you can practice. It requires pulling back from the world and spending some serious thinking on what is important to you, the principles you want to practice, the values you want to express, how you want to treat others, what you need to do for others to treat you the way you want to be treated, what you want your life to mean to the world, and how much discipline you are willing to invoke to achieve your goals. Being intentional helps you avoid confusion and false starts, or being scattered in your thinking and activities. It enables you to live a conscious life.

I ran the half mile on my high school and college track team. In the high school state finals I had a slight case of the flu and stopped after the 3/8 mile mark. I really could have kept running and 50 years later I am still not sure why I stopped. I rue that decision to this day and it stands out to me as an example of my lack of intentionality about that race.

Act when you know it is right to act so you don't have to look back with regret. But when you fail to act, forgive yourself and learn so you don't fail again.

Here's a suggestion that will help you think with more intentionality. I have a friend who wanted to quit smoking but he said, "I can't quit smoking." Like all of us, he can, of course, do almost anything he decides to if he applies the proper motivation, thought, and effort to it. If he says "I can't quit smoking", something else (smoking) has control of him. But if he says "I won't quit smoking" (as if it is his intention to smoke), it implies he has control over it and it becomes a much more intentional act. Now he has to think from the perspective of "Is it really my intention to smoke? If it is not my intention to smoke, I have a little more power over it and maybe that is the boost I need to quit." If you have something you want to do but are saying "I can't", change it to "I won't". This makes it easier to say "I will" and change your intentionality.

Corollary: *Plan your work and work your plan.*

Corollary: *Live so you do not have to look back and say "I should have—."*

BLOCK 18. Happiness is your responsibility and yours alone.

I once said to a married friend, "It's wonderful to see how happy Mary (his wife) makes you". His immediate response was, "Worth, I'm happy to be with Mary, but she's not responsible for my happiness. I and I alone am responsible for my happiness and then we can be happy with each other". And it's true. Happiness is my responsibility and I need to accept that responsibility. That's not to say you can't rely on your spouse to help you work your way through a blue funk or a difficult situation. You're there to help each other. Remember that "For better or worse" deal? But ultimately you are responsible for making yourself happy.

CONDUCTING YOURSELF

BLOCK 19. Take risks. Think outside the box.

Taking a risk means taking a chance, making an attempt at
something, or trying something about which the outcome is in
question. I once called a competitor to see if I could sell a client
of his a product (at the customer's request). I did not know this
competitor at all. I did not know whether he would laugh at
me and tell everyone he knew I was an idiot. I did not know if
he would call his client and tell him to never speak to me again.
When I called, the competitor paused and said "Why don't you
come over and we'll talk about it." We met for three hours, and
nine months later I became his junior partner, significantly fast-
tracking my career. I took a huge risk with my ego, and it turned
into one of the major turning points in my life. What did I have
to lose? A little ego, and, as stated previously, that will grow back.
And by the way, he taught me to regard events that could be
interpreted as threats as opportunities. He went on to become
one of the great mentors of my life.

You can't plot and plan every move in your life. But coura-
geously inserting yourself into unknown circumstances where
you have no idea what the outcome will be will often bear fruit.
It may take time for it to happen, but just wait patiently.

In 1971 someone invited me to a Toastmasters club to learn
public speaking. Even though I had spent 18 months as an officer in Viet Nam and had had several leadership experiences, I
hesitated because I was afraid of speaking in front of audiences.
It is said public speaking is feared more than death by most
people, so I reluctantly accepted because I realized I needed it.
Four years later I was the District Governor for the state of
South Carolina for all Toastmasters and had become proficient
at speaking. In 1977 I started a new club when I moved to

53

Pittsburgh and it still exists today. Several hundred people have now moved through the Toastmasters experience and become more adept at a life skill because of me, and it all started when I realized I needed to do it because I was afraid of it. By the way, a corollary benefit was I met lots of people in a city I was new to whom I would otherwise not have met. Other professional benefits happened for me from all those new relationships that were developed.

Corollary: *The opportunities in your life will expand geometrically with the number of people you meet and interact and the number of experiences you attempt. This is a critical habit to adopt if you are going to expand your opportunities.*

Corollary: *You create your own opportunities.*

Corollary: *It's not just what you know, it's who you know, and that's a function of how many you know.*

Corollary: *As an example of thinking creatively and outside the box, connect the nine dots below with 4 straight lines without lifting your pencil from the paper. The answer is on page 157:*

```
    ·     ·     ·


    ·     ·     ·


    ·     ·     ·
```

BLOCK 20. Develop a sense of controlled urgency.

This is a paradoxical suggestion, isn't it? What I mean by this is that it is useful to have a sense of completing tasks at a good pace without creating an abundance of stress in your life. It's quite a balancing act with the guideline of living within the moment, isn't it? But a sense of urgency is necessary if you are going to fulfill your potential.

You only have twenty-four hours a day and you can use them wisely or foolishly. Moving through them too slowly will reduce the number of experiences and opportunities you have.

BLOCK 21. "I need your help."

This is one of the most powerful phrases I know. I have noticed that when I use this phrase, people almost always become more alert and attentive to our conversation. Most people respond to it very positively and will want to hear how they can help. If the request is reasonable, they almost always are willing to proffer the help for which you are asking (unless you are asking to borrow money. That's a little dicier.) Of course, there are people who will look at it as your admitting you are weak or vulnerable. If that is your read of their personality, be prepared to deal with a negotiation.

BLOCK 22. You only have one chance to make a first impression. Use it well.

Because he had to take his three children somewhere later, a man whom I did not know brought them to a meeting I was attending. I shook hands with him, and then he introduced me to his ten, twelve, and fourteen year old. I enjoy meeting young people, and I always wonder how they will handle an introduction to a strange adult. Upon being introduced, each of them held out the right hand, looked me in the eye and held my gaze, and gave me a firm handshake. They did not try to pump my hand up and down hard, they didn't drop their eyes from mine, they didn't hand me a limp fish as a handshake. I knew they had been taught how to meet people, and that created a good impression not only of them but also of their father. Imagine his pride when I reinforced them by saying "I want to compliment each of you on how you met me. You had a firm handshake, you looked me in the eye, and you created a really good impression of you and your dad by doing that."

Notice I haven't identified the gender of these children. This is just as important for girls as it is for boys. You only have one chance to make a first impression and these are the two most important elements for anyone to learn about how to create a good impression. It's easy to teach. Just take a few minutes to point it out to the seven year old in your life and to practice it. It will pay him or her dividends the rest of his or her life.

THREE

Faith

....

"He who has faith has... an inward reservoir of courage, hope, confidence, calmness, and assuring trust that all will come out well—even though to the world it may appear to come out badly."
—B.C. FORBES

> **BLOCK 1.** You can't have evil without good, but you can have good without evil. Choose good. It helps grow your soul, reduces your stress level, and makes life more enjoyable for you and those around you. Practicing good helps you and thereby the entire world. Practicing evil eventually brings misery to everyone, yourself included.

I have good friends whose son graduated from college recently. Four years ago, as his mother was giving her son one last goodbye hug when they delivered him to school, she whispered in his ear, "My son, please guard your soul". What an incredible balance of request and admonition! It requests (instead of demanding), that he tend to the core of his being. It asks that he avoid evil. It asks that he think about his actions and thoughts with the uppermost consideration being how they impact his care for the most important part of himself. I am sure they had a conversation along the way whereby she explained what she meant by this request. She has continued to say this to him each time they part to reinforce its importance. If each of earth's 7 billion people thought like this, would there be any evil in the world?

BLOCK 2. Pray like the outcome depends on God, work like the outcome depends on you, and do them both at the same time.

God sustains us through difficulty and gives us hope. I believe we have gifts of intellect and other aptitudes provided by God which he expects us to apply to better the situation of ourselves and others. He is the senior partner and we the junior partners. If I rely on him to sustain and to guide me and I stay centered through prayer and meditation, and if I work hard and apply the gifts He has provided, my outcomes will be to the benefit of others and me. Sometimes I meet with defeat. But if I keep applying my gifts, all will turn out well in the end.

My wife, Janet, is a wonderful practitioner of this guideline. She is one of the hardest workers I know for the projects and causes she supports, and she often engages herself and others to commit to a 30 day prayer regimen to ask God's support and intercession in her efforts. It's a powerful combination to use, helps you keep God at the center of your efforts, and enables you to have good without evil.

And speaking of prayer, there are three types of prayer: prayers of thanksgiving, prayers of mercy, and prayers of discernment. One of the three of these is always appropriate depending on your circumstances.

Corollary: *Evil destroys your hope. Don't let it win.*

BLOCK 3. "We are called to answer the prayers of others."

These words were uttered by a minister on a Sunday about 60 seconds after we arrived late for services when he was already in the middle of his sermon. I have heard many other words of advice or observations in my life but these have stuck with me like glue. When I remember to, I try to evaluate my actions against this maxim. Even a kind word or acknowledgement of another person's presence or existence can be an answer to prayer. Just think: 60 seconds later and I would never have heard these words that are such a strong mantra. What a blessing!

Question: How can you put this into effect? Kevin Elko is author of "The Pep Talk" and three other books and a nationally known motivational speaker. I interned for Kevin in 1995 for a Masters in counseling and we've remained friends since. Recently he said,

"Worth, I prepare myself every day to intentionally do good in the world."

"How do you do that, Kevin?"

"When I leave my home I prepare to look for opportunities by saying to myself 'Lord, let me be a blessing to someone today'. It reframes how I look at the world and the attitude with which I approach my day. It keeps me on the lookout for reaching out to others".

I started doing this and you know what? It works! I find myself being more sensitive to what's going on around me and looking for opportunities to help fill people's needs or address issues they face. The first day I said this little prayer, I stepped outside my comfort zone and helped a lady with a parking problem. It only took 30 seconds but she was grateful and I felt really good about myself.

You don't have to do big things to bless others, although you may need to step outside your comfort zone and inconvenience yourself a little. Sometimes the simple act of acknowledging people's existence with a nod or a friendly hello is a blessing.

Try it. I <u>guarantee</u> that if you do this for two weeks, you will find yourself being a blessing to multiple someone's each day, you will feel lighter in your spirit, and you will hold your head a little higher. Your self-image will benefit significantly also, regardless of your station in life.

Corollary: *Your faith is most strongly evidenced by your conduct.*

Corollary: *Servant leadership is assuring other people's highest priority needs are being met.*

Corollary: *The better angel in you will stand if you allow it. (Kris Kristofferson)*

Corollary: *A good source of self-esteem is doing things others find useful or helpful.*

Corollary: *What we do here echoes in eternity. (Russell Crowe in "Spartacus")*

Corollary: *What you give you keep forever.*

> **BLOCK 4.** If you are still alive on Earth, your mission continues.

No matter what your condition, even if you are physically or mentally impaired, you are still playing a role in life. It may only be teaching others to have patience and to care for someone, but you are still contributing. You are setting the tone with your response. Kay Yow, a legendary coach for the women's basketball team of N.C. State, had a 21 year battle with breast cancer, and I once saw her on TV coaching a game. She looked terrible and she was weak, but she was still helping her girls play the game. That experience will stay with those women the rest of their lives, and when they encounter tough times, they will stand on her shoulders and respond with strength and courage. You can do the same and serve as an example of how to respond in bad circumstances.

Incidentally, this is what I mean when I say "People absorb us" and "More is caught than is taught". She never said to her players, "Look how brave I am being by continuing to coach you while I feel terrible and am dying". She taught them by her behavior, not her words, how to handle adversity in their lives. You do the same thing everyday with those you love and those with whom you are in relationship. *What are you throwing?*

Corollary: *We teach what we are.*

BLOCK 5. Marry someone of your own faith. Marriage is difficult enough as it is without different religious beliefs entering the equation (rearing the children, where to go to church, etc.)

Let's face it. Marriage is one of the most refining, challenging, and rewarding undertakings in the human experience. But the art of marriage is a lifelong and sometimes difficult road, requiring frequent compromise and adjustment to the other person's peccadilloes and value system. There are more than enough compromises to be made without having to figure out how to accommodate a significant difference in religious beliefs. If both of you are unwilling to convert to the other's faith, think long and hard before marrying, especially if you plan to have children.

BLOCK 6. Ask people "how's your faith walk?" You may change a person's life.

Although over 90% of Americans say they believe in God, the practice of faith has been waning for decades. You don't have to wave a Bible in people's faces to express concern about the role faith plays in their lives. Faith can provide a touchstone of security and assurance and centeredness in people's lives. You may be the person to help them discover or re-discover it.

BLOCK 7. Trust in God in good times and bad. Never be ashamed of your faith.

It's easy to turn to God in the bad times or emergencies when you most need help. Most people say their faith grows the most at those times. It's harder to practice your faith when times are good. Give thanks regularly when you are in the good times, because bad times will appear when you will need help. Maintain your connection with God at all times.

> **BLOCK 8.** A truly happy person is one who can enjoy the scenery on a detour. Live simply. Love generously. Care deeply. Speak kindly. Leave the rest to God.

If you can do this, you will succeed at living in the moment and getting the most enjoyment from it better than 99% of the humans that walk the planet. We are such a helter-skelter and rushing world, especially the Western World, that we focus a great deal more on what we have to do next or say next rather than what we are doing now or hearing now. Living in the now also enables you to be a better listener by not trying to formulate your responses while the other person is still speaking.

BLOCK 9. The gift is in the wound.

This one is hard to understand for most people, including me. When we experience life's wounds (failures, losses, attacks from others, betrayals, bad decisions), it is sometimes easy to wonder why God allowed them to happen to us or even to blame him for them. I'm not a theologian by any stretch of the imagination, but I like Harold Kushner's explanation in "When Bad Things Happen to Good People". There are all sorts of risks and temptations on our physical plane: accidents, physiological maladies, genetic abnormalities, addictions, distractions, and so forth. Sometimes bad things happen just because they happen as a result of this being a physical existence and the risks involved with that. Sometimes they are self-inflicted. But when they just happen, it's because that is the nature of this physical existence, not because God inflicted them on us.

The question for me is not so much where the responsibility lies as what I do with the circumstances and how I respond. There's the story of the woman who lost a son at an early age. She wondered for years why God had allowed this to happen. But instead of becoming embittered and separate from God, she became one of the most compassionate, caring, understanding person whom people knew. She turned her wound into behavior that understood the pain of others and was able to help ease them through their pain.

Your wounds can help you in the same way. Whether the wounds are happenstance or self-inflicted, you can reach out to others to help them with their wounds, and by doing so, heal your own wounds.

BLOCK 10. When God doesn't give you what you want, maybe it's a blessing.

In 1999 several of my friends and I had been on a mission trip to Uganda and decided to start a coffee farm to create jobs and self-sustaining income in an area that had 65% unemployment. By 2002, we had prepared and planted a 25 acre coffee farm with its associated infrastructure (well, water tank, irrigation system, storage building, etc.). That same year we were really criticizing ourselves because we failed to raise enough money to mulch the coffee in preparation for the dry season.

Shortly thereafter we received an e-mail from our manager Thad Cox that said, "We have had a miracle. A farmer some distance from the coffee farm started a fire to burn off two acres in preparation for planting a crop. A fifty mile wind sprang up causing the fire to burn out of control, racing the two miles to the coffee farm. Because the ground was bare, there was no fuel for the fire to feed on and we did not lose one coffee tree of the 11,000 seedlings we planted. Praise God we were not able to raise the money to mulch."

This experience taught me that sometimes when I don't get what I want, maybe there is a good reason. It has made it easier for me to accept difficulties in my life, and to move on when things don't go my way.

BLOCK 11. A letter from God to you:

My Beloved Child,

I have created you to express me, to know me, to be me. All life on your planet earth is a training school for the purpose of becoming aware of me, your Father and your God.

My kingdom is a finished kingdom. You are not aware of it.

Now is the accepted time. My way for you is a perfect way. I have given you freedom of choice as to the manner in which you will walk in my way. You may turn to me and let me guide you into patience, pleasantness, and peace leading you by the pressure of my hand on yours, or you may find the way by the trial and error method, by pain and hard struggling, or by breaking your heart on the rock of my law. That is not the way I desire you to go. I would pick you up in my arms holding you close and sheltering you from the storms, from the stony trail, from your lonely desert walks.

Whatever the earthly trials, whether they are long or short, the real meaning will only bring you closer to me, closer to reality, and eventually into divine union with me. This is my way for you.

From: Nancy K Helms, Mother of Carolyn and Worth Helms

After her death, I found this among some papers in an old file typed on a sheet of paper with my mother's ancient Remington typewriter. I don't remember if she gave it to me or if she claimed she wrote it herself. It could easily have come from her, however, because she was a writer and she thought like this. If it did not come from her and she copied it from someone, my apologies to the author for not giving him/her credit. It sounds like her philosophy, although she never expressed it verbally to me. At any rate it is a beautiful expression of how God would have us proceed with life and relationship with him. May you find it within yourself to accept and follow his will and hopes for you. And thank you, God, for granting our mother peaceful rest several years ago.

Corollary: *Faith is not about everything turning out okay; Faith is about being okay no matter how things turn out.*

FOUR

Financial Guidelines

. . . .

"Your net worth to the world is usually determined by what remains after your bad habits are subtracted from your good ones."
—Benjamin Franklin

BLOCK 1. Happiness is positive cash flow.

Isn't it a good feeling to have extra dollars in your bank account at the end of each month? Contrast that with the feeling of running out of money a few days before payday and having to borrow from your in-laws or a friend (whom you may already owe from last payday). The extra dollars at the end of the month happen if you discipline yourself to take on only the obligations you can afford and to save some dollars each month to create the means for future needs.

There will come a time in life when everyone's cash flow will depend on his/her habits of saving money toward the time they retire. This only happens if young people are taught to save a part of their income each month, whether it be from an allowance when they are young or from earnings when they are older.

Teach them to set aside 20% of their allowance when they are young toward a future goal of something they want to buy. Then teach them to evaluate using the money to purchase something today versus continuing accumulating their savings against a future desire. My son began mowing lawns when he was ten to save money toward buying a car. When he was 16 ½ he bought a used Toyota Land Rover for $5200. I'm sure there were many temptations along the way, but he stuck to his goal of buying a car. By the way, he sold the car three years later for $8200, so he learned to search for value through this process.

People learn 90% of their financial habits and behaviors not from their banker, insurance agent, or investment advisor, but from their *family of origin!* You are already teaching your children or grandchildren their financial habits with your own behavior. Are you setting them up with healthy financial behavior for life?

Corollary: *Pay yourself first. Save some money each month through your 401(k), or whole life insurance from Northwestern Mutual, or a disciplined investment commitment. I've used good quality whole life insurance (as well as other vehicles) and have been quite pleased with my outcome, flexibility, and multi-purpose functionality. I've used the cash value in my insurance a number of times, and always paid it back to myself so it would be there the next time I needed it.*

Corollary: *Try to save and pay cash for wants or needs.*

Corollary: *Use credit cards to get the points and discounts, but pay them off every month. Paying interest to a credit card company is a stupid use of your hard-earned dollars.*

BLOCK 2. Never give up more than 49% of your company's stock.

If you are an entrepreneur, keep control of your company while you are building it. You are the one with the ideas. You may need to hire management help to implement and market those ideas, but never give more than 49%. When you can sell it to someone for more money than you ever imagined, then you can cede more than 49%.

> **BLOCK 3.** Don't put all your money into intangibles, like stocks and bonds. Buy real assets too.

There are three principles in real estate purchasing: location, location, location. Similarly, there are three principles in investing: allocation, allocation, allocation. You should <u>never, never</u> "put all your eggs in one basket". Believe me, I tried it and it doesn't work. Be sure to develop an asset allocation formula with which you are comfortable and which considers your risk tolerance (allows you to sleep at night). Include an appropriate allocation to real estate, art, precious metals, and other tangibles.

Corollary: *Start early to give your money a long time to accumulate. Time will pass much faster than you think it will.*

Corollary: *90% of your investment return comes from asset allocation, 10% from the specific investments you pick.*

Corollary: *Financial accumulation is a marathon, not a sprint. Most of us must rely on time and reasonable returns rather than hitting home runs to accumulate money. If you save $1,000 per year for 45 years at 6%, you have over $225,000. Compound interest is a miracle. Let it work for you.*

BLOCK 4. If you are going to invest with someone who is not publicly traded, do a thorough check of their background. Emphasize their past actions, behaviors, and history ten times more than their words. Spend money to hire a detective to check them out. It won't cost much relative to your investment.

I once invested with a man who had 4 private partnerships. I learned about him from a highly respected investment newsletter. I talked to the editor who knew him personally and who invested with him. I talked to people in the community about the advisor. He had a PPM (Private Placement Memorandum) prepared by a highly reputable 400 lawyer firm. I met with the investment manager 3 times personally.

Seven years after I began investing, I received a call that the man had left a note on his desk that all the money was gone and he was fleeing. He was eventually tried and went to jail for 14 years, and I was lucky to have some of my money returned. It was a painful learning experience and played havoc with my ego.

I thought I had done a thorough enough investigation of the man, as did 350 other abused investors, many more sophisticated than I. It is obvious, however, that he was able to deceive lawyers and skirt regulatory agencies, and I needed to do an even more in-depth investigation of his background.

Corollary: *Trust but verify.*

BLOCK 5. Never be ashamed of earning a lot of money. The more you have the more you can help those less fortunate than you are.

I have always believed in helping others. Once I have enough for my family's basic needs and have provided for the contingencies in my family's life (death, disability, retirement, education for children, etc.), I have the opportunity to seek out organizations which are efficient at helping to fulfill the needs of those less fortunate than I am. I personally like to find organizations that weave into their mission helping others to permanently improve their lot.

For example, I could never have helped start the coffee farm mentioned in Faith-Block 10 if I had not saved extra money to help seed the startup of the farm. We bring the coffee to the US and sell it, and all profits are used to drill water wells in Uganda, replacing mudholes as the water source. Using our profits and donations, to date we have drilled over 75 wells, providing fresh clean water to over 75,000 people The villages in turn are required to collect a fee from users to accumulate a maintenance fund and learn to self-sustain a community asset.

But I could not have done that if I had not made some extra money to channel in that direction. I'm pleased I was able to amass enough to reach out to help those less fortunate than I. We helped some desperate people to improve their lot because a number of us made a little more money than we needed.

Incidentally, we calculate that every cup of our coffee that people drink provides 300 cups of fresh water over a ten year period. See the video of the farm and buy our coffee at ugandangold. com. Thanks!

BLOCK 6. Don't fall in love with real or personal property so much that you make bad decisions about buying it.

Your keeping an objective mindset in purchasing, whether property, clothes, cars, or anything else, is critical to good decisions. Letting your emotions rule you in these situations can lead to bad decisions that have long-lasting consequences.

Corollary: *Don't let your competitive instincts cause you to make bad purchasing decisions at auctions.*

Corollary: *Don't let your love of bright shiny things overwhelm your reason.*

BLOCK 7. The first law of economics is "There ain't no free lunch". Make sure you are getting what you pay for. Look under the hood to see if the motor is as good as it sounds.

As much as I wish there weren't, there are charlatans in the world. They will take advantage of you if you are too naïve, especially in this electronic age when deception can be practiced so impersonally. Your best line of defense here is to do business with people with whom others have had a good experience. If you need a service, ask at least two good friends whom they use to provide that service and pick the provider you like best. There is always a cost to something and you need to determine what that cost is before committing. Be what I call "Trustingly skeptical".

Corollary: *Always look a gift horse in the mouth.*

Corollary: *Always get a second and sometimes a third bid.*

BLOCK 8. If you lend someone $20 and they never see you again, it was probably worth it.

'Nuf said.

BLOCK 9. Be yourself and don't try to keep up with the Joneses.

Competition is one of the most powerful motivators of human behavior, but it can drive you to make some decisions that are just plain dumb and have damaging results. Make sure your commitments are within a budget you have set for yourself and not driven by other unhealthy impulses.

BLOCK 10. Never accept free tickets for sitting through a time-share presentation. The dynamics are against you.

In 2008 we went to a time share presentation to get two free $75 tickets to Disneyland. I told my wife we would not be buying a time-share since Orlando is only 2 ½ hours from a condo we own already that is totally paid for. You already know the rest of the story. We bought the time share, and I made one of the bigger mistakes of my life. We actually ended up paying someone to take it because in 2010 you could not give this thing away. If you really want a time share, google "timeshares for sale" and the name of the city, and you'll find plenty at 1/4 the price of a new one. Offer them ½ what they're asking to start the negotiations. If they laugh at you, call someone else.

BLOCK 11. Don't buy new cars unless you want to lose 15-20% when you drive off the lot. A certified low-mileage car will cost you a lot less (remember cash flow?), be a truer value, and give you as much pleasure. It's not usually an investment, it's transport.

I know someone has to keep the automobile industry vibrant, but it doesn't have to be you. I have bought 3 new cars in my life, and each time it was because of ego. That's not a good rationale for spending extra money that will disappear from your personal financial statement as soon as you drive off the lot. Every other car I have bought has been used, and I have gotten as good and long service from them as I have from the new ones. One car had 75,000 miles on it and I paid $16,000 for it. I sold it 9 years later for $2300 and it had 252,000 miles. I could have bought new cars along the way but it's not nearly as cost efficient as buying used. Most millionaires do not buy current model year cars.

BLOCK 12. Avoid debt. When you have debt, someone else owns you, your time, and your income.

There are three rules for managing your debt:

1. The amount you borrow should be reasonable relative to your resources and ability to repay. Know what sacrifices you have to make and are willing to make to afford the payments.

2. From the very beginning a plan should be in place to repay.

3. Repayment should be the primary commitment of your resources, even over personal spending desires.

In 2009, my wife and I experienced a significant financial reversal. I had created some debt from another asset I owned to put into an investment that went sour. Re-paying that debt, even though it was to myself, became my top priority over vacations and luxury spending. It was difficult, but we righted the ship and moved on.

Corollary: *Deficits, whether personal or national, DO matter.*

Corollary: *If you don't have a plan to control debt, it will control you.*

BLOCK 13. Tell your children occasionally you cannot afford something they want. Use this as a moment to teach the concept of saving for a need or a desire.

I have a friend who saw three empty cookie packages in the garbage one day. He asked his wife how many packages a week their four kids were eating, and she replied ten. He asked her to buy three per week, and when the kids asked why there weren't more cookies, she was to tell them they could not afford any more for that week. He had plenty of money and could have bought all the cookies they wanted. But he wanted to teach them the concepts of limits, scarcity, moderation, and rationing. He wanted them to learn the ability to limit themselves so that if they fell on hard times, they would be able to adapt.

Corollary: *Deny yourself an occasional pleasure or desire to remind yourself that there are many people in the world who live subsistence existences.*

Corollary: *Take care of the pennies and the dollars will see to themselves.*

FIVE

Health

. . . .

"The greatest wealth is health."
—VIRGIL

BLOCK 1. Don't ever smoke.

My dad was born in 1908 and, as an adult, smoked two to three packs of cigarettes per day. He died in 1968 at 59 ½ from congestive heart failure before he ever had a chance to meet my son, his grandson. When I was leaving for college, he pulled me aside one day and said "I want to ask you to do something for me. I want you to commit yourself to not drink or smoke until you are 21. You can then make a decision, without peer pressure, whether you want to adopt either of those habits. I'm not going to promise you any reward for doing this, because you'll be doing it for yourself. You don't even have to report back to me whether you decide to comply with this request".

I had my first beer when I was 23, and I had a cigarette to my lips one time in Viet Nam when I realized it violated a belief I had developed. I loved my dad, trusted him, and listened to his request and honored it. Sometimes you do things because you trust the people who ask you.

Corollary: *Only put things in your body that do no harm to it.*

BLOCK 2. Get exercise for current enjoyment and to give you a better quality of life in the future. "Later" will be here sooner than you think. You may not think about having good health in your older age today, but when you get there you certainly will.

You don't have to be crazy about it or overdo it, but do moderate exercise to keep yourself toned and in good shape. Don't overeat. Eat good foods. Use fish oil to minimize inflammation in all the organs of the body. The payback is significant in later years when the body begins to fail just because of age. Not carrying extra weight around is so much more pleasant. Your body is a house for your consciousness and your soul, and your time here will be much more pleasant if you take care of it.

Corollary: *Money cannot buy health, especially at the stage of life when you have money. Take care of yourself. Eat a good diet and exercise moderately.*

BLOCK 3. Take one or two teaspoons of fish oil per day for general health.

In 2005 I was diagnosed with pharangeal throat cancer in the form of a 3" tumor. I began taking 4 teaspoons a day of high potency fish oil about three weeks before beginning 36 radiation treatments and chemotherapy. By high potency I mean each teaspoon had 1800 mgs of EPA and 900mgs of DHA, so I was getting 7200mgs of EPA and 3600 of DHA per day. (Make sure your fish oil is from cold water fish and purified.) My oncologist had no objection to my doing this. Fish oil is a powerful substance for fighting inflammation throughout the body (read Barry Sears **The Anti-Inflammation Zone** to learn more). They told me I would probably have to have a feeding tube, I would lose half my saliva glands, and I might lose around 20% of my body weight. After 4 weeks of radiation, the techs began asking me why the skin on my throat wasn't breaking into sores. I never needed a feeding tube. I never took the medication for dry mouth they recommended to me. I did go on a canned nutrition drink exclusively when I could not stand the smell or consistency of food in my mouth (VHC 560 from Nestles).

I only lost 17 pounds or about 9% of my body weight. Two months after treatment the doctors at the swallowing clinic put a camera down my throat and saw so little scarring they were asking if I had really had had throat cancer. Today my saliva glands work fine, my appetite is fine, and I have no residual effects except my voice dropped 6 notes and I get hoarse occasionally. By the way, I was on blood pressure medication when I began taking the fish oil and today I'm completely off of the medication and BP is normal. Fish oil is really good and powerful stuff. Take it.

SIX

Learning

....

"Let us never be betrayed into saying we have finished our education; because that would mean we have stopped growing."
–JULIA H. SULLIVAN

BLOCK 1. Learning is finding out what you don't know. Doing is demonstrating you know it. Teaching is expanding others into your realm of learning and doing. We are all learners, doers, and teachers.

Learning is always possible. It's the most important thing you do for yourself, regardless of age. At 53, I studied for a Masters in counseling to learn why I was making some of the mistakes I was repeating in life. It was very revealing and I met some great folks. I just became a mentor for an inmate at a county prison. I believe I will learn as much from him as he will from me.

Corollary: *Never stop learning.*

Corollary: *Put yourself in circumstances unfamiliar to you not only to contribute, but also to learn.*

Corollary: *You teach what you need to learn.*

Corollary: *There is a principle which is a bar against all information, which is proof against all arguments, and which cannot fail to keep a man in everlasting ignorance—that principle is contempt prior to investigation. -William Paley*

BLOCK 2. Remember your history: Where you came from, where you are going, and how you created this mess you are in so you don't repeat it.

The whole purpose of this book is to teach you some things I have learned through some difficult and some pleasant experiences, in hopes of helping you avoid the difficulties and experience the good. There will be experiences you have in life, however, from which you will learn other lessons that you will need to remember. Pass those lessons on to those around you. And remember the lessons you learn so you don't repeat the mistakes. If you repeat the same mistake twice and can't figure out why you are making it, find a good counselor.

Corollary: *Don't yield your future because of your past.*

Corollary: *Each of us has two lives: The life we learn with, and the life we live after that.*

BLOCK 3. Figure out what your "Experience Screens" are and how they effect your behavior and decision making. Try to take those "screens" into account and adjust accordingly.

From the day we are born, we "experience" life and the thousands (probably millions) of interactions and events that come with it. We interact with everything in our world---other people, objects, colors, sounds, touch, smells, tastes, circumstances, etc. Each experience usually has a positive or negative impact on us and some sort of emotional overtone. These are what I call "experience screens". The most important ones are our interactions with other people. For example, if I had numerous negative interactions with a relative, I would begin to interpret and respond to the world through eyes that are leavened by those experiences

I studied a case history of someone whose experiences with a person were so noxious that she began to lie to protect herself from the situations that arose with this person. Thus she developed an "experience screen" that taught her to lie anytime a situation became threatening or uncomfortable. This pattern became the dominant theme of her life even in relationships with others who were not threatening. Identifying and exploring your own experience screens will enable you to understand some of the major themes in your life and, if they are harmful or hurtful to you or others, allow you to change the impact that theme is having on your life. Since we often can't see the forest for the trees, a counseling process might help here.

That's what studying for the degree in counseling did for me. It enabled me to identify some of the "experience screens" that colored my perception of the world and affected how I reacted to current circumstances I encountered. You will ease your way significantly if you can enter into this process.

Corollary: *Identify and become conscious of the experience screens you have and try to counter them with healthier behaviors. Awareness is critical here.*

LEARNING

BLOCK 4. Learn to write (in English!) as well as you speak.

This is a crucial skill for success and advancement. Use your time in school to greatest advantage to develop this skill. You don't have to be a great author, but you certainly need to know how to communicate on paper.

Corollary: *Don't let texting be the only way you know how to write. It won't be acceptable in that corporate report and you will fail to advance yourself if you can't write properly.*

BLOCK 5. You will become wise and perhaps a little more humble when you realize how much you do not know.

Learning never stops. Sometimes lessons must be repeated and re-learned, and that is still learning. When you admit to yourself (and maybe others) you don't really have all the answers, you'll be a more humble and likeable person. I golf two or three times a week. No other game so closely replicates the cycles and ups and downs of life. I consistently have to go back and re-learn the things that were working for me until I became overconfident that I had the game licked and quit doing them. Life is the same way. When you start to think you have it licked, it will jump up and bite you.

> **BLOCK 6.** Those who do not learn from history are doomed to repeat it. Lunacy is repeating the same action over and over, expecting a different outcome.

After two failed marriages, I decided I was the only common factor in the failures. The two ladies were good people, so I must be a significant part of the problem. I went back to school and got a masters degree in counseling, and realized what I was doing that was counter-productive. I was seeing the world through one of those "experience screens" I described earlier. I did some self-talk to begin changing the screen and have now been happily and productively married to the same lady for fifteen years. The same thing applies to nations. Our children have to know our history so they can learn from our mistakes.

Corollary: *If you always do what you've always done, you always get what you've always gotten.*

SEVEN

Living Your Life

·······················

"There are only two ways to live your life. One is as though nothing is a miracle. The other is as though everything is a miracle."
—ALBERT EINSTEIN

BLOCK 1. There are only four things which you control when you waken in the morning and face the day:

1. Your work ethic

2. Your care for others

3. Your passion and enthusiasm

4. Your attitude

Most of us would like to have total control of every aspect of our lives. The reality, however, is that we can only control the above four aspects. To the extent we pay attention to these we have some control over outcomes. If you look at yourself at the end of each day and can say "I worked hard when I worked, I played hard when I played, I extended myself and was considerate of others, I showed enthusiasm for that which I believe, and I didn't give up in the face of adversity", you have had a day that was good.

Paying attention to these four things enables you to have the impact you wish to have. Can you imagine losing if you constantly practice these behaviors? Your work ethic assures your continued focus on your objectives and projects. Your care for others and compassion enables you to weave consideration of other people's feelings, needs, and perspectives into your decisions and actions. Your passion and enthusiasm help convince others of your sincerity and belief. And your attitude helps you face and overcome the obstacles and defeats that we all encounter. Focus on these four things and you cannot help but be a winner of a fulfilled life.

Corollary: *When the above don't work, remember perseverance.*

BLOCK 2. Life is a series of continual course corrections. Intentional, values-driven course corrections will benefit you much more than simply reacting to circumstances.

We are all continually making decisions. Decisions are either proactive or reactive. Proactive decisions are well thought out, take into account the values wiring of the decision maker, are based on reasoning, and take into account potential consequences. Reactive decisions are not well thought out, usually are full of emotion laden rationales, and don't adequately consider consequences. If you practice the latter type of reasoning, you are like a pinball being knocked all around the pinball machine not knowing where you are going next. But if you practice the proactive style, you will have a lot more control over your outcomes.

Corollary: *When in doubt, evaluate your intentionality to determine whether you are on the right course.*

BLOCK 3. The richness of the tapestry of your life will be woven by the people you know and the books that you read.

Make an effort to read good books and to know good people. They will both reinforce who you are and make you want to reach higher. Your possibilities and opportunities expand geometrically with the number of people you know. I cannot tell you how often in my life opportunities have arisen for me to cross-connect people for either business or personal reasons because I have taken a risk of interacting with a stranger or asking people what is happening in their lives. You will make a lot of your own luck by doing this. The publication of this book happened because of this. I never intended to write a book of any sort until the spark of an idea came from someone and I began asking questions and reading.

Corollary: *Always read stuff that makes you look good if you die in the middle of it.*

Corollary: *Pick three people you admire because of the traits they exhibit and copy three of their traits. Pick your friends the same way, just more of them.*

BLOCK 4. When you don't know what to do next, remember one word: Curiosity

This came from a professor of mine who taught this maxim in relation to the counseling profession, but I think it applies to every situation. Remembering it allows you to ask questions and develop alternatives no matter what your circumstances. It also allows you to ask question after question that probe to deeper and deeper levels of information out of which you will be more capable of forming responses or answers to situations in which you or others find themselves.

Of course, you need to maintain an awareness of appropriate boundaries when asking questions about personal issues. I always like to acknowledge the possibility I may cross appropriate boundaries by saying something like "If you feel uncomfortable with this conversation or this question please tell me and we won't pursue it."

> **BLOCK 5.** You must sacrifice boredom in order to live freely and happily.

Are you a sender to life, or a receiver? If you are watching TV 3-4 hours per day, you are a receiver. If you fill your hours with activities, outreach, and involvement in the world, you are a sender. You will have more impact on your world and leave a more lasting legacy if you are a sender. Get involved. Becoming mentor to a prisoner makes me a sender. There are some risks, and I'm not really sure how to do it, but it could really be important to someone. Get out there.

Each of us falls into one of three categories: We either make things happen, watch things happen, or wonder what happened. Which category are you working toward achieving?

BLOCK 6. Your primary obligation in life is to be true to yourself.

This means to know what your values are and to stand for them. Do things and make decisions with which you feel at peace— that is being true to yourself. If there is dissonance, you know something is wrong. Evaluate until it feels right, then move in that direction.

There are four questions people ask themselves:

Where did I come from?

What is my code of honor?

What am I doing here?

Where am I going?

I don't have a clue about the first (although I have some theories that I won't bore you with), and I really don't know the answer to the last, except I try to live my life in a way that I get to be with my loved ones who have gone ahead of me. What I do know is that I have total control about the answers to the second and third questions and you do, too. You and I both determine our code of honor and what we are doing here.

Corollary: *You can't be true to yourself without consciously listening to yourself.*

BLOCK 7. It may be that a big purpose in your life is simply to be kind to others.

Kindness is a hard-to-come-by commodity today. A smile, a wave, a warm greeting, or simply saying "Howdy" to a stranger you pass in the street can lighten someone's day and make them feel better. Try it. It will make you feel good, too. If people say at your funeral "He/she was always so kind and warm", you will have left a powerful legacy for them to follow.

BLOCK 8. Accept that some days you're the pigeon, and some days you're the statue.

Sometimes, regardless of how hard you try, you can't stop "stuff" from falling on you. Accept it, mourn the loss, then get off your duff and get back to work correcting the situation.

Remember my description of my experience with cancer? It was a detour I never expected to experience. Heart disease I was prepared for because of my dad's history, but never cancer. But after a few days of reflection, I felt that even though I never expected to have it and did not want it, it was an opportunity to experience something a lot of people travel through and an opportunity to show others what I thought might be an appropriate way to deal with it. I came back to this thought whenever I had doubts or wondered about why it had happened to me. It gave me an anchor to windward to steady myself and to ground myself when I waivered in trying to float above the experience.

BLOCK 9. Relish each and every moment of the activities you enjoy.

There are activities throughout my life that I have thoroughly enjoyed. For example, I was a competitive runner in high school and college, primarily in distance races. I have sung in choirs and individually for audiences since I was twelve. I love to play golf and am decent at it (although members of my leagues will take issue with that when they read this).

I can't sing anymore because of throat cancer in 2005, although my speaking voice is fine. I am unable to run long distances any more because of a lack of leg strength and my energy not being what it needs to be to sustain extended effort. I am still active on the golf course, playing about three rounds a week at a reasonably competitive level.

My point here is not to elicit sympathy from you for my basic inability to sing or run anymore, but rather to point out to you that I think I could have focused more on my enjoyment of those activities while I was able to do them.

I did not focus on that enjoyment as much as I could have because it never occurred to me that someday I would lose the ability and energy to do them. I have taken this lesson and applied it to my golf game. Someday I won't be able to do that either, so I am focusing at age 69 on getting better. If I don't, someday I'll look back and have to say to myself, "I could have been a better golfer". I don't want that disappointment.

Corollary: *The joy is in the doing. Relish every moment of it.*

BLOCK 10. Listen to your heart.

Janet and I were married in 1996 when I was 53 and she 42. She agreed to marry me knowing that at my age I did not want children, even though she did want them. She accepted me on those terms but said she would pray that my heart would change. The decision to marry was an outstanding one and we were very happy with how well we our lives and personalities fit with each other.

In 1999 we joined 17 friends and strangers on a short-term mission trip to Uganda, having no idea what we would do or why we were going. Our primary motivation was to return to Africa after a wonderful photo safari we took to Botswana in 1997. Little did we know how life-changing that mission trip would be.

We were in a gathering of about 4,000 people in the market square of Hoima conducting an evangelistic outreach and Janet was singing from a makeshift stage on the back of a tractor-trailer rig. I looked down and there was a 6 year old African boy gazing up at me, so I reached down and picked him up so he could see the stage. He was quite comfortable in my arms. I looked around and saw 10 or so children surrounding me all dressed in the same color clothes. At the end of the event, I set him down and we went on our way.

Later we visited an orphanage, and the boy, Paul, turned out to be a resident. When we visited the orphanage, we met a 7 year old girl named Olivia. She was charismatic, one of the leaders of the kids, spoke English very well (it's the official language of Uganda although many people speak one of their 50 or so dialects), and she was a singer like Janet and me.

After two visits to the orphanage, I said to Janet, "There's something I want to talk about." She responded, "I have something I'd like to discuss too. But you go first."

"Okay", I said, "Here goes. I think perhaps we should consider trying to adopt Olivia."

Janet's mouth sagged open, tears filled her eyes, and she said, "That's what I wanted to talk about"! We had both come to the same conclusion at the same time! It's stunning how often one of us will open a topic and the other one will respond "I was just going to talk about that!"

We tried for two years to adopt Olivia and failed. After two years we decided to help her in Africa, and found a wonderful family for her to live with while we sent her to boarding school. As of this writing we are working on entrance for her into an American college so she can be here in America with us. We communicate by phone and e-mail, and Janet returns to Africa periodically for visits with Olivia on missions she has developed. We listened to our hearts and Janet's dream for a child was fulfilled in ways neither of us would ever have imagined.

That mission trip changed our lives in more ways than one. I helped start the coffee farm which has impacted thousands of lives, and Janet decided to obtain a Masters in Evangelism and Missions, has developed and led a program to heal orphan hearts of the pain they feel from their circumstances, and has started a Christian school in Northern Kenya.

> **Corollary:** *You never know what's around the corner until you take a peek.*

> **Corollary:** *Listening to your heart can change your life in ways you could never imagine.*

EIGHT

Personal Disciplines

....

"If we don't discipline ourselves, the world will do it for us."
—WILLIAM FEATHER

> **BLOCK 1.** If something goes wrong, look in the mirror to see if that person is primarily responsible. After assessing the culpability assignable there, you can look elsewhere if further search is necessary.

I have noticed that our society is characterized a great deal more today by rationalization and denial of responsibility than it was when I was being raised. Harry Truman said "The buck stops here", referring to the phrase "Passing the buck". When we all get back to taking responsibility for our actions and the actions of those in our charge, our country will return to being the beacon of hope for the world that we once were. Look at yourself first for responsibility. Accept it. Then make the situation right.

Corollary: *When you are wrong or make a mistake, admit it to the persons involved and apologize. You will be respected for your integrity in admitting your error, and for accepting responsibility for your actions. That is the starting place for reconciliation and solving the problem.*

BLOCK 2. Don't try or not try. Do or don't do.

I made the comment to a boss of mine once, "I'll try to do that, Sir." His immediate response to me was, "That's not enough commitment from you, son. I want to hear you say you'll do it". I found it interesting that he cast it in terms of commitment. If I only say "I'll try", I will always be able to say I sort of succeeded because I tried. That's not good enough. Saying "I will" is much more of a commitment and a positive approach.

BLOCK 3. Don't confuse activity with achievement. To have achievement and to progress, you must measure the results of your activities.

That same boss once said to me that he saw a lot of smoke in what I was doing but he wasn't sure there was enough fire. There was a lot of activity, but he wasn't sure I was achieving anything. Ever notice someone who is always busy, but doesn't seem to accomplish much? I'll bet they are not measuring the results of their activities. If you aren't measuring your results, how will you know what you have accomplished and when you've reached your goals? Start measuring and I'll bet you start to see some changes in your behavior and in your outcomes. There's that accountability thing again.

Set measurable goals for yourself in any effort you are putting forth. Keep records about how you are performing against those goals. That will tell you what you are actually accomplishing. I was in the insurance business, and a lot of people thought their success depended upon their technical knowledge of the products they sold. The real determinant of their success was their prospecting skill and their courage to hear people say "No" and to make the next telephone call or appointment in the face of rejection. I was trained to keep records every day of how many phone calls I made for new appointments, how many appointments I actually had, the number of fact finders I obtained, the number of closings I had, and all the other activities reflective of good prospecting efforts.

Each week, all I had to do was to look at my records of my prospecting activities against my goals in each of those categories to know if I had performed well. If I was prospecting adequately, the sales would come. I had to match this effort with good technical skills and integrity in dealing with people to fully succeed, but no success would have occurred had I not measured my success in the prospecting activities required.

By the way, I defined integrity as advising clients to do what I would do if I were in their same circumstances. That's why I was able to work primarily from referrals, because people felt I would be honest with them.

BLOCK 4. My father once told me there were two things he wanted me to practice forever: Always be honest, and never panic. Those two words for living have stood me in good stead since age twelve, at least twice saving my life.

I think I have talked enough about the integrity and honesty issue in other sections. The don't-panic admonition is extremely important, too. If you panic, you are more likely to make irrational decisions that make the situation worse, or you can freeze and do nothing, which is just as bad. Keep your head, think, tell yourself to stay calm, and you'll stay in a much better response mode. Other people can do it and so can you. Panic is the enemy of rational response.

Janet and I were fortunate enough to take an African photo safari to Botswana once, ending our trip at Victoria Falls. We decided to raft the Zambezi River below the Falls, with its Class 4-6 rapids. On the second rapid, I was thrown clear, but then was dragged back under the raft. My kapok life jacket was rubbing against the bottom of the raft and the water was pressing me up against it as we sped through the rapid, and I could not move. My Dad's words "Don't panic" echoed in my mind. I was running out of breath and was about to take in a lungful of water when it seemed God breathed more air into my lungs. I wasn't panicky and I think that helped sustain me a few moments longer. Those moments gave the raft time to hit another rapid, bouncing off the water, and I was able to dislodge myself and push out from under the raft into sunlight and air. Never panic! Thank you, Dad.

How do you avoid panicking? The best way I know of is to try to stay aware of whether you are panicking, and to remind yourself continually to think, think, think. Notice I did not say,

"Don't be fearful". Fear is okay because it creates adrenaline and extra energy to deal with circumstances. But don't let the fear turn to panic. And the best way to control that is to think about alternatives to work your way out of the situation, evaluate them, and put the best one into effect. Panic prevents you from being able to think.

Corollary: *To rob panic of its control over you, think.*

> **BLOCK 5.** Time works hard when hard work doesn't. Sometimes a situation needs to age with an occasional nudge for a desired outcome to occur.

There are times that, no matter how hard you work, you can't move things forward. This is when patience comes into play, and you force yourself to wait until circumstances are more favorably aligned to allow you to push things forward again. Perseverance and patience are wonderful partners in your arsenal of traits to practice.

My partners and I once prospected a large corporation ten years before we finally hit on the correct approach to obtain a contract with them. It was one of our biggest successes and the relationship continues to this day, even though I am out of the business. And even though I helped obtain entry to the client, others were more responsible for different aspects of the case than I. The whole was definitely greater than the sum of the parts in that instance.

BLOCK 6. You are successful if you are happy and content with your life.

Someone once said to me "Happiness is wanting what you have, and having what you want." The question is, what do you want? Do you want material things? How much is enough? Do you want rich relationships? What is a rich relationship? Do you want fame and public recognition? Is recognition in your local community enough or do you want national notoriety? Would it make you happy to just be contributing to the well-being of your fellow man without recognition? Figure out what will make you happy, and see how you feel when you have it. We have a tendency to never be satisfied. But when you feel happy with what you have, stop and enjoy it for a while, and then see if you want to re-visit your needs.

BLOCK 7. Precision and neatness count.

I called a company the other day to pay a bill, and I said to the clerk "You have the most beautiful handwriting. It makes a wonderful impression for your customers." She was very appreciative, of course, and went on to tell me how she developed it. I listened because I was interested, and I'm sure the next time I call she will remember me and help me willingly. The point is, she created a very favorable image of her company and its products with just her handwriting. You also create an impression on people and impact their confidence in you by how you present yourself in writing and by being precise. You don't have to be anal-retentive about it, just make it part of who you are.

BLOCK 8. Trucks and cars sometimes have a governor to control the speed of the vehicle. You can think of your values as the governor of your behavior and decisions. Write your values and what is important to you so you can evaluate your decisions and actions against them. This enables you to assure congruity between your actions and decisions and your values. If there is ever dissonance between your decisions and/or actions and your values, you have to change one or the other. (This is one way of practicing intentionality).

There are a lot of things you can write about to develop your values code: loyalty, integrity, honor, truth, courage, kindness, morality, stewardship, orientation toward others, spirituality, cleanliness of speech, listening, how you make decisions, philanthropy, health, education, ambition, walking on the light side rather than the dark side, etc. We did this for a 450 employee non-profit of which I am on the board, and the values have now become so ingrained that we don't even have to look at them to test our decisions. You can do the same thing for yourself personally. If you consciously know where you stand and have written it down, these values will automatically act as the "governors" of your life.

BLOCK 9. Bad news doesn't get better with age. Confront it as soon as possible.

When you have bad news to deliver to someone, whether it is about a business issue, an organizational issue, or a personal issue, confront it as soon as possible. People can deal with almost anything except uncertainty and surprise. In business we called it "falling on our sword". For example, if you cannot complete a commitment, tell the other party as soon as possible. The earlier you tell them, the more time they have to develop contingency plans to deal with the fallout. If you can't pay your mortgage, call your bank immediately and begin working out an arrangement. Waiting three months will only make the situation worse. I did not know it, but I was practicing this when I went into the house to tell my mother I had bent the tongue of the trailer (See 3 under Relationships). The longer you wait, the less credit you get for being forthright and having integrity, and that can only damage the relationship further.

The same thing applies to personal relationships. Allowing problems between yourself and someone to fester doesn't solve them, it only allows them to grow worse.

Corollary: *You can't change other people. But if you change the way you deal with them, they may change.*

NINE

Organizational Principles

....

"It is not a question of how well each process works, the question is how well they all work together."
—FLOYD DOBENS

> **BLOCK 1.** Hire people who are good raw material and have exhibited integrity and a desire to work hard.

Back in the days when I was hiring people, I tried to assure myself that candidates for employment knew how to learn, were motivated, and had integrity. When I stuck to those three characteristics, I always picked a winner.

Corollary: *Try to hire people who can grow to replace you. Many times you will only get the next higher job if you have a replacement available and have exhibited the ability to renew the organization by recruiting and training qualified people.*

Corollary: *As you become more successful, become more attuned to those around you in order to maintain and make relationships with those you can really trust.*

BLOCK 2. The most effective and enjoyable form of management is derived by practicing the maxim "He supports that which he helps create". Give others a participative voice, recognizing that ultimately someone must take responsibility for making the decision.

This is a very powerful principle and will make you an outstanding team leader and team player if you have the patience to do it. When were you more enthusiastic and dedicated to your job—when someone told you what the plan was, what your role was in the plan, and how to carry out your part, or when someone gathered the team together and gave them a voice in what the goals were, what the plan was, and the role each person was to play? If people are given a voice, they will work harder, longer, and more willingly than they will ever work if they are treated as automatons. It may take a little longer to work the process, but I'll bet you the plan will be better and you will have an incredible team effort as an outcome. Try it. Hire a facilitator if you need to.

Corollary: *The whole is greater than the sum of the parts.*

Corollary: *If everybody wins, it's not as important who gets the credit.*

BLOCK 3. Humor improves the environment when you conduct a seminar, lead a group, or make a speech. It will refresh your audience and keep their attention by providing a fun moment of respite from concentration on the subject.

If you really want to keep your audience's attention, inject a little humor every 4-5 minutes in your talks. Humor is an excellent relief to concentration, and it makes the time seem to go faster. You don't have to tell jokes. Tell something funny that relates to the topic. Make a quick quip about a point you just made. The only time you don't have to do this is when you are teaching students who will be graded on what you are imparting. However, they will appreciate it, too, and will think you are a better teacher for it.

BLOCK 4. A task will expand to fill the time allotted to it.

This is a corollary of Murphy's Law, which is "If things can go wrong, they will go wrong". When someone tells me they have been to a four hour meeting, I can almost always guess that there was no agenda with specific allotted times for each topic. Things seem to wander on and on in these circumstances and suddenly four hours are gone. Plan the time you think it will take, allot the time, and stick to it. You'll be amazed how efficient you get. I know one person who conducts meetings with no chairs to encourage people to be concise and to the point.

Corollary: *When conducting meetings, remember "The mind will absorb what the rear will endure."*

BLOCK 5. Before making a decision, look at the other person's point of view to see if any part of it has merit and can be woven into your point of view.

Nobody is right all the time, including you and me. Use those listening skills we talked about earlier. You might be 90% right, but if you listen to the other person, maybe the two of you will be 100% right.

BLOCK 6. The two most powerful motivators in human behavior are recognition and competition.

This is really important in organizational motivation. Why do you think sales organizations call people's names for outstanding performance? Why do you think goals are set for people upon which to be evaluated? If you use these two motivators in a healthy manner, you'll get a lot more performance and better team work from your staff.

Corollary: *The sweetest sound in the whole world is that of my name.*

BLOCK 7. Once you have made the sale, shut up.

This applies anytime you are trying to convince someone, whether it's in sales or personal relationships or business settings. Continuing to convince someone after they accept your argument can actually lead to their reversing their agreement with you and it certainly wastes time. I learned this from the president of a company to whom I was making a presentation. He had been nodding his head in agreement with everything I said, but I kept on and on making my points. He finally raised his hand in a gesture that said "Let me speak" and said, "Worth, do you know what I do when I think I've made a sale?" Not knowing his point, I said "No Sir", and he responded "I shut up".

Bam! Right between the eyes he hit me with a great piece of advice. I learned then when people agree with you, move to the next level of the process or the next item on the agenda. This applies all the time, in personal interactions as well as in business.

TEN

Relationships

....

*"Personal relationships are the fertile sand from which all advancement...
all success, all achievement in the real world grows."*
—BEN STEIN

BLOCK 1. Don't be reckless with other people's hearts and don't stay in relationship with people who are reckless with yours.

Being careful with other people's hearts is important not only for how they feel about themselves, but also for how you feel about yourself. Don't damage others by manipulating them, taking advantage of them, or abusing them in any way. There is enough hurt in the world without you adding to it. Think about what you are saying or doing and its impact. Acting in a manner calculated to get what you want without taking the other person's feelings into account is just plain mean and without decency.

There will be times that you start down a path and make commitments or say things with the best of intentions, but events turn in a way that is not acceptable to you. In these circumstances you have to be honest even if it hurts the other person. Just do it gently and in private, please.

BLOCK 2. Tell your spouse five positive statements for every one negative statement. If you slip to a two to one ratio, your marriage is headed to difficult waters.

I learned this just recently, and boy do I wish I had learned it long ago. Positive reinforcement is so important in a marriage. If we aren't careful, we will accentuate the negative rather than the positive. I think that is because the negatives (and we ALL have them) are the things that irk us and cause friction. If you can say five positives to each negative, I'll bet things will brighten in your marriage within thirty days. Try it. I'm still working on it. Ask Janet.

Corollary: *When Momma's (Daddy's) happy, everybody's happy.*

Corollary: *You are only as happy as the most miserable kid in your family.*

BLOCK 3. Never overreact when your kids tell you something or behave in a way you don't like.

When I was 15 years old, my father assigned me the chore of burning in our pasture a pile of pine saplings we had cut off of our property. My mother would back the trailer to the pile with our car and go in the house while I loaded. Every time I needed the trailer moved I had to walk to the house to get her to drive the car. On one of the trips the trailer was a little far away from the pile, so I decided to back it up a little without going to the trouble of walking to the house. It was a '47 Plymouth straight stick.

I had never driven, but I had watched and it seemed simple enough. I started the engine, put in the clutch, geared into reverse, and started engaging the clutch. Apparently my foot wasn't on the clutch very well because it slipped off and the car flew backwards since I had revved the gas much too high. The front wheels of the car were apparently turned because the trailer immediately went at a 90 degree angle to the car, bending the tongue of the trailer at 45 degrees on the bumper of the car.

I killed the engine and stumbled shaken and scared to the house to confess the accident to my mother. Very angry, she immediately said I would have to deal with my father about this and called him at work and put me on the phone. I confessed what I had done and the first words out of his mouth were "Are you all right?" The conversation from there on was very even-tempered and rational. He said I would have to work off the cost of the damage the rest of the summer, and forgave me.

We had a long conversation when he came home about using good judgment in deciding what to take on while still trying to be aggressive and trying new things. We talked about the sort of things I needed to get experience at before I took them on by myself.

His reaction has stuck with me the rest of my life. I learned a lot about how to respond to life's trials with that experience. Your offspring will handle kids the same way if you do this.

BLOCK 4. Help your children choose their friends carefully by asking them to bring them over for dinner.

Would you let your kids hang out with a bunch of criminals? How will you know what your kids friends are like if you don't spend time with them? One of the best ways to do that is to invite them for dinner. You'll see what sort of manners they have, how they talk, and have conversations to learn a little about them. It's also fun!

BLOCK 5. If people say "To be honest", "Trust me", "Frankly", or "To be perfectly candid", does it mean they are lying to you the rest of the time?

I know people who use these phrases way too much. The phrases mean nothing if you have integrity and honor in the first place, and I try to avoid ever saying them.

The difficulty here is that most good people want to believe other people are good and mean well toward us. We want to believe they are being honest, and if they say they are to be trusted, it encourages us to trust them. Since we already want to trust them, we are set up to believe what they say. If there's a way, corroborate from another source what they are telling you.

Corollary: *Trust and verify.*

> **BLOCK 6.** Emphasize humility rather than pride in your approach to relationships. Don't brag.

When he was 5, I took my son to play Putt-Putt, and he parred the second hole. As we approached the third hole there was a boy about his age waiting with his father, and my son said to him, "What did you get on that hole?" The kid said something like a four or a five and my son promptly said "I got a three", with a lot of emphasis on the word "I".

There was no one behind us so I walked him back about twenty steps with me and we had a calm conversation about what bragging was and how it made other people feel about themselves and how it distances you from others. Today he is 35 and owns a company he started. He's a good marketer, and he'll tell you what he can do, but he doesn't do it in a bragging manner. He talks about that lesson still.

I was able to teach this lesson because I experienced it myself. When I was 29, my boss called me into his office, closed the door, invited me to sit and then said "I don't quite know how to say this, but apparently a lot of people around here think you're an ass." My mouth sagged open, my eyebrows went up, I turned beet red, and I became speechless. He went on to say he wasn't sure why people felt that way, but I should examine my behavior to see how I might be creating that impression. Perhaps I was parading my education too much, or I wasn't listening to others, or I was dominating conversations too much, or I was indirectly bragging. He wasn't sure what I was doing, but he asked me to look at myself and reframe how I related to people.

Six weeks later he invited me to his office again and closed the door and said "Worth, I've never seen such a change in a person.

You're much more congenial, you've lost the military command attitude you seemed to carry, and you seem much more open and relaxed. I had not noticed it before but you are different. Good job". His having the courage to give me straight feedback and my ability to hear it without becoming overly defensive had a profound impact. I was then able to pass this lesson on to my son.

Being confident in who you are and what you accomplish can be expressed with either pride or humility. If you express confidence pridefully, it creates distance between you and others and can make you appear arrogant. This can easily make people dislike you, or not want to be around you, or even not want to work with you. On the other hand, if you express confidence modestly, most people will admire you for the way you handle your success. You can have a good self-image without expressing a big ego.

Humility is the opposite of pride. Pride and humility cannot coexist. If you reduce one of them it's as if a vacuum is created, which nature abhors, and the vacuum becomes filled with the other trait.

Pride comes from ego, and boasting or bragging comes from pride. How do you control your pride quotient? We talked about this in a discussion group, and one member said he used EGO as a acronym for "Easing God Out". Since he wanted to lead a life that honored God, whenever he sensed himself becoming prideful, he controlled it by reminding himself that he did not want to ease God out and that being humble is a way of allowing God in. He felt any of his accomplishments were a result of the gifts God has given him, and to be prideful about those gifts or the outcomes attributable to those gifts was to dishonor God. He was an accomplished man, but he related like an everyday guy. It worked for him, and it can work for you and me and those we teach.

BLOCK 7. Structure your true family to include those with whom you have a bond of respect and joy in each other's lives.

Janet and I have a fairly broad network of friends and acquaintances with whom we share joys and sorrows to keep our relationships alive. It adds to the richness of our lives and to the support we can rely upon when we need it. This is where the real meaning of your life lies, in your relationships. Value those relationships, and tell people you value them and love them. I've even said I love you to some of my close male friends. I have a friend who recently died, and I regret not saying it to him.

Corollary: *Your dismay and sadness at "Goodbye" will turn to joy at your next "Hello".*

BLOCK 8. If you have to correct someone, do it in private and do it constructively.

I can't tell you how important this is. No one likes to be corrected in front of others. It's embarrassing and shaming. I imagine you don't like it so why would anyone else? Correct people gently but firmly in private, tell them what you expect, and move on. Leaven it with praise for something they do right. I've seen some pretty horrible examples of the wrong way to do this on the sports field with seven and eight year olds. Don't do it.

BLOCK 9. If you have the strength to forgive, you have a greater ability to love.

You can have more love in your life if you can forgive. I think this is one of the toughest things to do in life and requires lots of stepping above yourself and your ego. Forgiving does not mean you have to be in relationship with someone. It just means you forgive them and move on without bitterness or hatred for them. If you can do that, it probably means you do have a pretty good capacity for love.

BLOCK 10. They may forget what you said, but they'll never forget how you made them feel. Strive for the latter in your relationships.

This one points out what is really important in human relationships: feelings. If you can be even-keeled in your responses to others and act in a kind manner, you'll be remembered for that. Oh sure, you'll be remembered for what you did in life and your accomplishments. But what they'll talk about at your funeral are the things that made you human and how you related to others. I think I'm fair at this, but not nearly as good as I could be. Guess I have more work to do on it.

Corollary : *The most fulfilling rewards in life are given to those who bring joy to the existence of others.*

Corollary: *If you can't be kind, at least have the decency to be vague.*

> **BLOCK 11.** Use the three R's, Retreat, Rethink, and Respond, rather than the one R, React, to manage your response to situations.

I learned this as a technique for managing behavior when I was in some counseling situations. If you just react, there is a much higher likelihood you will respond out of one of those experience screens we discussed earlier. The other alternative is to give yourself a little time (Retreat) to ponder (Rethink) the situation, and to develop a better thought-out action or reponse (Respond). It's like the old count-to-ten maxim except this tells you what to do while you are counting. You really don't have to count all the way to ten. Just be intentional about your responses rather than reactive.

Corollary: *The difference between responding and reacting is about three seconds.*

BLOCK 12. Practice patience with others and yourself.

This one I probably will have to work on the rest of my life. Impatience distances you from others and requires them to constantly forgive you. I don't like to feel I have to be forgiven for something, and you probably don't either, because it usually means I have done something wrong. Since I don't like that feeling, I can avoid it by stopping the behavior that causes it in the first place. Be patient with them. Give them, and yourself, a chance to correct the mistake and to do better the next time. Janet is being very patient with me as she teaches me patience. She's modeling it.

RELATIONSHIPS

> **BLOCK 13.** Tell your spouse and children you love them every day.

Janet taught me to do this, too. Every time we speak on the phone or say so long for the day, she wants to do this. She is one of the most positive people I know, but she says you never know when something might happen, and we won't see each other again. She wants each of us to remember that the last time we saw each other ended with "I love you". Your kids need to hear it so they will carry it on in their adult lives. It is important that this be reinforced often, because in the helter-skelter of our lives, it is easy to lapse into the habit of not saying it at all. And it really is nice to hear, isn't it?

BLOCK 14. Love means saying you are sorry and asking forgiveness.

There was a saying around in the seventies or eighties, "Love is never having to say you're sorry". I never really thought about this until recently when I realized love was exactly the opposite of that. The old saying assumes forgiveness is automatic and doesn't need to be asked for. That's not the way human nature works. We are feeling individuals. If you verbalize the fact that you are sorry and request forgiveness from that person, you are reaching out to them and they have a chance to forgive you and grow closer to you. Try never apologizing to someone and not asking forgiveness for years and see if the relationship grows closer or further apart. You know what will happen.

BLOCK 15. If someone is doing a significant job for you at your home (painting, replacing a roof, landscaping, etc.) bake them a pineapple upside down cake or a pie (don't buy it, bake it) and brew some coffee, and they'll go the extra mile for you. Always ask if they would like coffee or ice water. Show them where the bathroom is when then arrive so they don't have to ask. Every time I do this they say it's the best place they ever worked.

I've had workmen say they don't want to leave our house, or even offer me a job because of this little bit of kindness. They always do a good job and I always feel good about myself. It's a Win-Win. What could be better?

BLOCK 16. Check out your potential spouse's family background carefully—divorce, broken homes, alcoholism, drugs, health history. This is significant baggage for you to help carry if your intended has not dealt with it. Observe the way the family members interact with each other because that is the pattern your intended will likely follow with you. That being said, hormones and chemistry are hard to fight.

Open and honest conversations about this are very important. We all carry baggage around with us and you will have to help your mate carry his/hers and he/she yours. It's better to know what the baggage is and to try to lighten it a little before you commit to each other than to go into a permanent relationship blind. Go to counseling before you marry and figure out where the potholes are in advance. Your life will be easier and more enjoyable for doing that. A lot of people don't do it because they are afraid they'll discover things that will upset or even terminate the relationship. But believe me, it's a lot better to find out in advance.

BLOCK 17. Pick battles that are big enough to matter and small enough to win.

This is under personal relationships because I want to apply it here more than anywhere else. Sometimes it is just better in your relationships to keep your mouth shut than it is to argue your point. Unless the fate of the free world depends on it, just let your wife go ahead and buy the yellow bed sheets even though you told her you preferred the aqua. You won't even see them most of the time because you're asleep. The rest of the time they are covered by the comforter. Move on to the important things.

BLOCK 18. Don't burn bridges behind you. You may need to retreat someday, and you may need that bridge to be intact.

This is one I have not had to learn from bitter experience. I seem to have intuitively known how to do this and have succeeded in leaving most of the bridges I can think of in place. How do you do this? Leave with as little rancor and harsh words as possible. If the other person is being harsh, do not respond in kind. Let their words roll off you. They are responding out of the hurt they feel. Do not allow bitterness to creep in. Take responsibility for your share of the severance. Apologize. Time will heal the wounds.

When I left jobs for other opportunities, I explained my reasons and asked for understanding. They all asked me to stay in touch. One job I left, I had been paid a draw. As I understand it, I was the only person to ever pay back the part of the draw for which I was responsible. This was the one time the boss was a little bitter, but I did what I was supposed to do to complete my commitment. My conscience was clean and he and I were cordial to each other after that.

BLOCK 19. Determine where your needs differ from your spouse's and develop compromises to fulfill those needs.

This is best illustrated by a couple of examples. Janet loves to have surprises at Christmas and therefore loves to give surprises. I like to tell her what I want for Christmas because it's practical and I derive joy from having what I want rather than receiving gifts that I won't use or that make no sense to me. I like to give gifts the same way. The two approaches appear to be mutually exclusive leaving room for no compromise. But we found a way.

I give Janet gifts that are surprises but not fulfilling my need for practicality. She gives me gifts I have asked for, fulfilling my need for practicality, but not fulfilling her need to give surprises. We are both joyful and grateful for what we receive, and we both surrender giving in the way we want to. Compromise.

Another example: Janet loves to weave the story with all the accumulating details with a resounding conclusion, and I'm a bottom line person who likes to get to the conclusion quickly. How to resolve these competing mindsets and needs?

She agreed she would start the story and soon tell me the end results, filling my need for the bottom line. I agreed to listen to the details after hearing the conclusion to fill her need for telling the story. If we don't do it this way, I'm squirming in my chair interjecting all kinds of questions which frustrates her in her story telling. This compromise enables her to tell her story with my full attention to the details, and we both get some of what we want.

Corollary: *It's better to have your needs partially met than it is for both of you to be totally frustrated.*

BLOCK 20. And last but not least—

A lecturer, when explaining stress management to an audience, raised a glass of water and asked "How heavy is this glass of water?" Answers called out ranged from 1/2 to 1 pound. The lecturer replied, "The absolute weight doesn't matter.

It depends on how long you try to hold it. If I hold it for a minute, that's not a problem. If I hold it for an hour, I'll have an ache in my right arm. If I hold it for a day, you'll have to call an ambulance. In each case, it's the same weight, but the longer I hold it, the heavier it becomes." He continued, "And that's the way it is with your stress. If we carry our burdens all the time, sooner or later, as the burden becomes increasingly heavy, we won't be able to carry on. As with the glass of water, you have to put it down for a while and rest before holding it again. When we're refreshed, we can carry on with the burden. So, before you return home tonight, put the burden of work down. Don't carry it home, you can pick it up tomorrow. Whatever burdens you're carrying now, let them down for a moment. Don't pick them up again until after you've rested a while."

Corollary: *Give yourself a break.*

Having a Conversation with Your Child or Grandchild

Talking and relating with a child or grandchild is one of the most pleasurable activities you can do. Additionally, I am always amazed at how quickly children pick up and understand concepts. These two factors make it easy to chat with kids about the concepts you have read above. As of this writing, I'm about two years away from having a conversation with my grandchild, but I do have experience talking with nieces and nephews. It is amazing how quick they are to understand concepts, and the vocabulary they have at age 5 or 6 is simply astounding. From that age on it just gets easier to communicate ideas and concepts to them.

Here are some suggestions for broaching the ideas, truths, and principles included in this book:

1. Look for behaviors or actions that trigger one of the concepts, and use it as a jumping off point for a discussion.

2. Plan a time once a month to take the young one out for a milkshake to talk about one of the topics.

3. Discuss the "Foundations" in an age-appropriate manner.

4. Don't underestimate the ability of the young child to understand the topics. They grow and learn so fast these days, plus it's an opportunity to expand their thinking. I am constantly amazed at the ability of my seven year old nieces to understand and verbalize concepts.

5. Ask a question to open the topic.

6. Dialogue back and forth is important rather than just telling them a concept. That will involve them more and let you check along the way if they are following the conversation. You'll be surprised how much your grandchild may already know.

APPENDIX

Here are a few examples of having a conversation with a child you're trying to teach:

ABOUT BRAGGING

"Timmy, I noticed you talking to the boy ahead of us. That was nice of you to do. What did you talk about?"

"Well, I asked him what he got on that last golf hole."

"And what did he say?"

"He said he made a five."

"And what did you tell him?"

"I told him _I_ got a three."

" Well, I'm sort of curious. How do you feel when someone tells you they are better than you?"

"I guess I don't feel very good. It makes me a little sad."

"Does it sort of make you feel ashamed that you didn't do as well as they did?"

"Yeah, I guess so."

"Do you know what it's called when someone says they did something better than you did?"

"No."

"It's called bragging or boasting. When you brag or boast to some one, it sometimes makes them feel bad about themselves. When you bragged to him about your golf score being better than his, he might have felt bad. I know you don't want to hurt people's feelings, so it would be kinder if you didn't brag about

155

yourself. But if someone asks you how you did on something and it turns out you did better, that's okay because you didn't start the conversation by talking about yourself. But you still don't boast that you did better. Do you see what I mean?"

"I think so Gran'pa. If I tell people I'm better than they are, it's bragging and might make them feel bad, so I shouldn't do it. But if they ask me how I did on something like a test and I did better, that's okay since they asked me. But I still shouldn't boast I did better."

"That's right, m'boy. You certainly understood that quickly. I'm proud of you."

ABOUT INTENTIONALITY

"Michael, do you know what intentionality is?"

"No Sir, what is it?"

"Intentionality is when you do something on purpose, you mean to do it, you intend to do it. Do you understand what I mean?"

"Sort of".

"Well, let me give you an example. Let's say your birthday is coming up, and we want to celebrate. That's an intention. We intend or plan or have a goal of celebrating your birthday. That intention or goal started out with a thought of knowing your birthday was coming up. So we plan to have a party with balloons and food and ice cream and cake and presents. It all started out with a thought and that turned into an intention. *You* have intentions all the time, you know."

"Really? How?"

"Well, you intend to play soccer this afternoon with your team, don't you?"

"Yes, Sir."

"You intend to go to school tomorrow, don't you?"

"I don't really want to, but, yeah, I'm going".

"You intend to eat supper tonight?"

"Sure".

"There you go. You have all sorts of intentions, don't you? And something else to think about: You can have good intentions and bad intentions. Good intentions help you or others, and bad intentions hurt you or others. So a bad intention is something like saying 'I'm not going to brush my teeth tonight'. It's bad because it hurts you to not brush your teeth. Or another bad intention would be to say to yourself, 'I'm going to pull Susie's hair'. That hurts Susie, doesn't it? But a good intention is something you do that helps you or others. So, for example, when you say 'I'm going to go practice soccer', that's a good intention because you'll help your team and yourself by practicing. When you say 'Mom, I'll take the groceries in for you', that's a good intention because it helps someone even though maybe you'd rather be doing something else.

Let me give you an example of my own. When I get in my car to go anywhere, I say 'Lord, let me be a blessing to someone today'. I *intend* to be a help to someone. Our whole life is made of intentions, and the more good intentions we have, the better life we can have. See what I mean?"

"I think so. I should do things because I want to do them and I mean to do them.

"That's great. It's really important for us to think about our intentions because they have such an effect on you and those around you. Thanks for listening, Michael."

ABOUT PANIC

"Johnny, what does the word panic mean?"

"I don't know, Grandad."

"Well, let me ask you this. Have you ever been scared?"

"Uh, yes, when I couldn't find Mommy in the grocery store."

"That's a great example. It's okay to be scared, because that tells you that something is happening that you need to do something about to help yourself or others. Sometimes when people get real scared, their fright is so bad they do what is called "panic". They panic so badly and they get so afraid that they can't think. Panic can make you feel so upset, or confused or flustered that you sort of freeze and can't think what to do. When you get in a situation like that, it's really important to keep yourself calm so you can think about the best thing to do to help yourself or others get out of the situation. What did you do when you were scared in the grocery store?"

"I looked for Mommy first, then I went to the front of the store and told the lady at the counter I couldn't find my Mom."

"That was really good thinking. You didn't panic, did you? You thought about what you could do to help yourself, to get help from someone. You were able to think instead of letting your fear control you.

"Panic is never a good thing to do. Always try to stay calm in any situation, even if you're afraid, so you can think of the best thing to do to to make the situation better."

ABOUT THE PUZZLE ON PAGE 53

In order to solve this puzzle, you have to "think outside the box" and not be constrained by the directive "connect the dots", as follows:

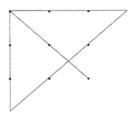

It's the same way in life. Sometimes you have to think "outside the box" in order to solve the issues you face. Don't let thinking within the box constrain you from developing solutions that creatively solve the problems you face.

Worth M. Helms

....

Worth Helms is a 69 year old with an array of background experiences.

He has BS, MBA, MSEd, and financial services professional designations. He was an officer in the US Army during the Viet Nam war serving 1 ½ tours there, and has experience in the corporate world. He owned his own business, and retired at age 50.

Obtaining a Masters in counseling, he helped counsel people with various issues on a volunteer basis. He has been to Uganda eight times on mission trips, and was president of a coffee farm he helped start there to create jobs and self-sustaining income. He currently serves on 5 boards of directors including a college, a large senior living facility, and a rehab program for prisoners. A throat cancer survivor, he enjoys golf, reading, current events and reaching out to others.

27964087R00093

Made in the USA
Charleston, SC
27 March 2014